A Letter to My Sons

Leaving a Legacy of Love

Chablis Dandridge

Liberty of Congress Cataloging-in-Publication Data is available on file.

ISBN: 9781091085916
Printed in the United States of America

Dedication

In Loving Memory of My Son

Jermaine "Snoop" Gamble
May 18, 1994 – June 6, 2014

This one is for you, Son. The sun set far too early on your journey. Only God knows why life deals us the hand we are dealt. Distance has worked against us. Time has robbed us. On June 6, 2014, whether we were ready or not, God called. I'll forever remember your fighting spirit. A generation apart, but both sons of the same struggle. Our hearts and spirits were, and are, connected by the same thread of energy that encompasses the message between these pages. I wish you didn't have to go so soon, but I thank God for the twenty wonderful years that we had you. Until we meet again, rest in peace— death will never do us part.

TABLE OF CONTENTS

Introduction

"I hate you, and I wish you would die!" These are the words whose power still haunts my thoughts so many years after they were said and thought forgotten. I am taunted by my memory at varying intervals through my lifetime and again.

The innocence of childhood affords us the passes necessary to live beyond the poisonous seeds we sometimes plant in ourselves as we develop. I still remember so vividly thinking those very hurtful thoughts as a child or even daring to utter them under my breath when I was angry at one of my parents. Of course, I didn't really mean it, nor would I have wanted either of my parents to ever find out that I had dared to even think it, but foolish innocence knows no shame.

I can happily look back on those tender years, glad I wasn't foolish enough to say what was on my mind. As an adult and now a parent myself thinking back, I'm disturbed by the idea that I could have been enough of an ingrate to even think the thought. All things considered, I made it through, and, as it goes with the life cycle, the tables have now turned. I'm no longer the immature youth, but the one who's responsible for taking care of them.

If the tenor of life is true to the idea that things happen in cycles and there is nothing new under the sun, I can bet my own kids have had similar thoughts about me. Something for which inexperience and youthfulness make concessions is known as egotistical bias as known in educational psychology. When children have not yet developed the skills to conceptualize that a larger world exists beyond the one they have created in their minds—an effect we soon grow out of but a sentiment I have not managed to escape, nonetheless.

In truth, it's embarrassing to admit that I have ever thought such things, but I am able to painfully live with it. What is seemingly unbearable, though, is the idea that my own children may have once felt that way about me, and I may have given them all a number of reasons for doing so.

How would I feel if I knew that any of my children felt that way about me? It is not a question I'm fit or prepared to answer. I would like to hope that none of my boys feels that way about me, but in the absence of a definitive answer I would have to assume that my children have their own sentiments about our relationship that I may never know. This is bearable. What is not is living with the guilt of never having lived up to a father's obligation to his children. While I may never know how each of them feels about me, I know perfectly well how I feel about them. I love them all.

As parents we make an unspoken, unconscious pact with our offspring to love, protect, shelter, guide, and care for them throughout a lifetime. It's obligatory. No one should have to tell us that this is our duty. A lifetime of symbiotic parent-child relationships, as examples, should have defined it for us long before we cross the threshold of parenthood ourselves. Even if we lack a complete family experience, there are enough models of it around us for us to know that parenthood is a silent agreement we make with our children the moment we become aware of their conception.

I would hope that none of my boys have the "I hate you, I wish you were dead" sentiment about me, yet I know I have come up very short of fulfilling a fraction of my obligation as a man and father. I could not be offended or upset if one of my children did harbor such sentiments. I have made many mistakes that I'm sure have caused all them a tremendous amount of personal grief. It has taken a very long and painful journey to manhood in my own life to become awakened to the reality that I have loafed on my obligation and an even longer time to realize that I'm still here and my commitment is far from over.

To these young men I would say, "I still owe you the best of all I have to give." No matter how much I've caused you all to lose thus far, I still owe you the debt of setting a healthy example of what manhood is all about. These are lessons that I should have shared long before now, things I should have been there to say at your tenth birthday party. I should have been at your junior varsity football game to share with you the lesson of strength and courage when you did something that took real courage. It is the conversation I should have been there to have when you were rounding that corner of puberty and anxious about your first sexual encounter.

I can't go back and make up for those experiences that I missed. They have all passed us by. I cannot change the mental and emotional damage that was caused by my absence in those so critical times in your lives. Those are moments we will never get back. What I can do is make sure you know the man I've grown to become and share the things I've learned in my own life that have taught me the values I now hold dear.

Time and distance have caused us not to be able to share the most important thing life has given us—each other. I have no one to blame but myself, and it's alright if you all blame me, too. It was my responsibility to ensure you all were provided all the elements you needed to grow into strong, healthy, balanced, and happy men. Somewhere along the way I fumbled, and life dealt us a blow that no child should ever be forced to endure. I can only hope that the content of these pages will somehow serve to fill in some of the missing places in your lives that have long gone empty and unfulfilled.

At this stage in your lives, you should all know me just as well as I know you. Only the opposite is true. Incarceration has kept me away for a decade, and, instead of knowing each other, we are more estranged than close. And so, because of the distress I've caused us, we've had to endure growing together under some very strenuous circumstances. Be that as it may, I am no more excused from my duties as a parent and a man than the parents with whom you have grown up.

I am still responsible for setting a good example, providing direction when it is needed, contributing some element of mental and emotional stability and support, and modeling the defining characteristics of manhood. I'm not sure how you all remember the past, or if there is any clear recollection of the type of individual I was or am. I can only tell you that, although my actions in the past may not have provided the best examples of correct and upstanding behavior, I am a man of many values and virtues. That's why this exchange is so important. If you've ever wondered who I am or "what my dad is all about," these pages will tell you the complete story.

It is an answer to questions you may never think to ask. A confession that, even if you thought to ask certain questions, will undoubtedly be more frank, honest, and complete than any one question's answer ever would be, a declaration of love that could be made by no other means, a pledge of eternal allegiance that is long overdue. It is the best of the man I've become. It is a promise to continue in the way of being the man I now know that I'm supposed to be. Defining manhood is no easy task. Thus far, I've learned that it's a process of evolution that is never ending.

There is an African Proverb that says, "It takes a man and a woman to make a child, but it takes a village to raise it." I don't think that there have ever been truer words spoken. There was a point in my life when I fathered two children. Throughout my journey, I was blessed beyond measure to have many more children share my space. Each one of us were tied to the other by some invisible thread of the spirit that has held us together over time. It has created within us a family brought from different corners—from different origins to a place of union that defined the very essence of the maxim "we are one blood." We are all family.

Darrius and Eric, my biological sons, Brandon and Elijah, my stepsons. Jermaine my surrogate son, and Jorge my godson. And of course, Christian my little brother, the baby of the bunch. You all are all my children. This letter is drafted to you. I hope that in my life I have given all of you the love you need to become the men you need to be. I hope that none of you will end this life with anything less than a complete knowledge and whole internalization of my love for you. Biology gave me two, but God gave me the gift of so much more in all you.

There was a time during which I stood in proxy on your behalf as the guiding force. In my absence there have been others who have done in my place the same for you. It is into the fabric of life that we are woven together as one: one blood, one family, and one humanity. That's why, although these pages have been composed of our sacrifices, of our hardships, of our process of growth and struggle in our individual and collective journeys to manhood—it is a word of encouragement and direction to everyone else as well.

It is a message for my sons, my brothers, uncles, cousins, and friends or for any man in need of another perspective on manhood. The road to maturation is often a bumpy, thorny, and difficult path to find. It takes some amount of deliberate effort in order to navigate the uncertainties of the process we call growth in life. Healthy development in life is something like being the captain of the vessel of your life in the raging sea of your destiny and trying not to capsize the ship. These are my sons, and we are the village. It's high time we stop evading the call of duty as men and be the shining examples of what manhood is supposed to be.

WISHFUL THINKING

It seems like only yesterday that I was engaging in my first real experiences in just about everything; my first time coming into the knowledge that a boy was very different from a girl, my first desires to pull away from my mother and take my first real steps toward male independence, the day I arrived at the conclusion (all by myself) that real men are tough, my first bouts with peer pressure, that first drink, the first joint, my first girl—all memories that are so branded in my memory that they seem like the very core of my true beginning.

I am aware that I have been living my developmental process for the entirety of my life. Nonetheless, there is still this strong impulse inside me that drives my memories and my most deeply embedded behaviors back to a few key points of my past. It's almost like I can relive my entire life in a few memorable and impressive experiences, and the rest just serves as a backdrop for those coveted highlights I hold so dear even today. I'm not sure I understand why, but I think that something about our psychological makeup causes certain things that happen to us to have a more lasting effect than others. Whatever the reason is, I am convinced that 98.9 percent of the man I am today is a direct result of resolutions I made at each of those critical turning points.

It almost seems juvenile to admit, but in order to remain true to myself I have to be honest: Most of the man I am today is largely because of the kid I was yesterday. I don't mean that I haven't grown up or matured much since I was ten. I mean there are still lingering wounds that had such a profound effect on me that two and a half decades later I am still acting in the interest of avoiding that pain. It's interesting that most of the information that we have gathered through the study of human behavior places a large amount of emphasis on the earliest of a person's experiences. All said, childhood is the staging ground for preparing yourself for the rest of your life. Most of your most critical lessons you have learned by age five, and the rest seems to serve only to complicate matters. By five you've learned to trust, share, and work on your own. You've acquired common courtesy, empathy, sympathy, respect, self-worth and a number of other little ingredients vital to survival in this modern jungle of life. All the good and necessary qualities that are essential to healthy balanced living.

Thereafter, things tend to regress. In the next stages of development, you must learn not to be so trusting. You learn that you can't share with everybody, and that just because you are courteous, kind, respectful, empathetic or sympathetic,

1

not everyone else will be. It is a dual reality that we must master if we are to survive, excel and achieve in the world we live in.

That's why, as silly as I feel for being a man of my childhood, I'm equally comforted that there is some legitimacy to those seemingly unreasonable resolutions I made so long ago. One of my strongest resolutions as a man-child was that I would be nothing like my parents when I grew up. I spent much of my youth trying to live up to that one, only to come full circle and realize that there were no people in the world better than them to be like. Still, the process of evolution presented a learning curve so dangerously sharp that I almost didn't make it this far. Resistance bred rebellion. Rebellion birthed delinquency, and well, it's not hard to see where behavior like that will take a person.

I'll never forget one of the very first experiences, or series of experiences that really shaped the strong-willed determination I developed. My mother had withheld some information from me, fearing I was too young to know or understand its meaning. As a parent I can appreciate her desire to shelter her child from certain things, but as a child, that appreciation and understanding was not so easily reached. Years had gone by when I finally learned the truth of what she had been withholding. To this day, I don't remember what exactly it was that I found out. I only remember feeling like I had been lied to and a sense of betrayal and hurt.

Her intentions were good, but the results were devastating. It set in place an overwhelming feeling of distrust and caused me to be closed to the very person I should have trusted with my life. On the flipside of the equation, it prompted an almost unchangeable resolve in me that when I became a parent, I would never lie to or mislead my children. Even if the situation were far more complex than their ability to understand, I would always do my best to make them understand any, and everything, they had a desire to know. Was it the best course of action? I'm still not sure. All I know is, I have never wanted the trust factor in our relationship to ever be compromised.

It was that, and many other situations like it that have made me into the individual I am. Those major life changes that transitioned me from one developmental stage to the next. Ultimately, I felt that I was fully developed by about sixteen or seventeen, mentally and emotionally at least. No, I'm not the same immature brat I was in my late teens twenty years later. I've changed times over since those impressionable days. However, the disciplinarian I am was shaped back then. My tendency to be real, open, honest and frank with my kids was formed then. My want to be a stable and common place in my sons' lives began then. My capacity to pick up, love, and parent all children was born then. And twenty years later, all those things remain just the same as I prefixed them at ten, twelve, fourteen, seventeen and twenty-one years old.

Rose Colored Specs

It's funny that as a kid you rarely have a clear concept of half of the meaning of the things that are going on around you. Hell, sometimes the same is true on into adulthood, so it's understandable that a child hasn't half a clue. The true irony is, of course, that even after you learn the lessons of time and maturity, we still have trouble relinquishing those childhood resolves that undergird who we are and how we live in our present.

Growing up, I was one of the oldest children in my family. Many of my cousins were a lot younger than me and I loved being able to exercise my maturity by helping my grandmother, aunts and uncles with the duties and responsibilities of caring for the babies. I had a Cabbage Patch Kid when I was a tyke, but I relished the opportunity to help change the baby's diaper (the stinky ones too). I did everything else too, feed the baby a bottle, burp him, give him a bath, take him for a walk, put him down for a nap, and any other chore an adult would let me do. In many ways, I've been a parent since I was ten, at least in my own mind anyway. I knew as a kid that I wanted children and I probably made a silent promise to myself that as soon as I could I would.

I had fond fantasies of what a great father I would be. My sons would call me daddy. They would look like me, act like me and sound like me. They would have my last name and I would take very good care of them and make sure no one took advantage of them or hurt them. I would protect them from everything. Oh, how wonderful youth is. It gives us just enough of an imagination that we can dream and dream big. When my first child was born, I was all that I dreamed I'd be (in thought anyway). I was ten years old again and I couldn't wait for all those wonderful things to start happening that I had waited for, for so long.

I looked at his small features, his jet-black slicked down hair and his small frail frame and I knew things were going to turn out just as I has envisioned them so many years before. All those resolves came rushing back to me, and I took careful note not to omit one detail of all the things I has internalized until that point. I'll never beat my kid if he always tells me the truth. I'll always tell him the truth no matter how I feel about it. I'll never put him on punishment (something I stayed on from twelve until I ran away). Nobody else would beat him or I'd kill them. I was stark raving mad about some of the things I promised when it came

3

down to my little boy, most of which, I, in one way or another lived up to, to some degree.

Those were the days. I was young enough that foolishness was not a foreign occurrence, fool-hearted enough to believe that I was right within reason in everything I did. I don't know that I saw manhood outside of fatherhood. I certainly didn't think being a father made you a man. I was so idealistic that I felt when you reached a stage when no one tells you what to do you were a man. A man in my mind was permitted to have kids so that's what I spent my early teens trying to do and prove—that I was finally a man.

In all honesty, by fourteen I had gotten so unruly that there weren't many people who could tell me what to do. This was just the indicator I needed to confirm my manhood (in my mind at least). I was no more a man at that time than I was a father at the time of my first son's birth. But the one thing inexperience is good for is allowing you to be totally convinced of things that are not totally true. So just like I became a parent just days before I turned seventeen, I had become a man somewhere around fourteen.

Imagine how misguided I was. A little dumb kid trying to find his place in a mean, demanding, unforgiving, and callous world. Going from boyhood to manhood doesn't come with an instruction guide. The process is sort of like stumbling around in the dark looking for a light switch to help you make some kind of sense of it all. It's like total chaos and confusion from every angle, and right when it seems like it's all consuming—your eighteenth birthday happens, you're legally a man and that light you were searching for finally comes on and lights up the dark. Not that it makes everything clear, but it is a time when everyone else recognizes you as a man. When it does happen, (the clarity of autonomy) it reveals the complete mess you've made and it's time to start trying to put things back in order.

HINDSIGHT IS 20/20

"In our every deliberation, we must consider the impact of our decisions on the next seven generations." ~The Iroquois Tribe

Hindsight is 20/20 is probably the oldest way of saying "If I only knew then what I know now." If you are anything like me, you've probably spoken those words more times than you would care to admit. It's one of those things in life that falls in line with the "I told you so" philosophy. As I look back over the past events that have shaped my life, I find myself revisiting too many happenings that reek of both the hindsight saying and the "please don't say I told you so" disposition. I've finally concluded that life would have been so much easier if I had just been a tad bit more teachable early on. Oh well, as the saying goes I can't "cry over spilt milk."

The light of adulthood was a rude awakening for me. I had done so much in my adolescent years trying to prove my manhood that by eighteen I had almost stamped out my own existence. My quest for manhood was so confusing that even though I had exemplary examples of what real character was, the most profound shows of what manhood was all about, and many morals and values shoved at me, I still found a way to get very off track. Believing that manhood largely consisted of total independence, all my focus and energy were centered on, and around just that—independence. I seemed to have forgotten or overlooked the rest of the defining characteristics of being a real man; those like respect, responsibility, leadership, contribution and a slew of other elements that it is necessary to exhibit if you're going to call yourself a man and really live up to the definition.

It's not hard to see why the light of legal adulthood was such a messy affair for me. I had not properly cared for myself and my relationships, nor any of the other vital aspects of my development for that matter. Although I had just about as good an environment as any growing up, my race to 'grown' left me badly in need of developmental maintenance. Consequently, I made it all the way to manhood nothing more than a little boy in a grown man's body.

Being eighteen meant I no longer had to struggle for power inside the home with my parents. They both recognized I was grown now. It meant I didn't have to worry about going to school or what the consequences were if I didn't. No one could make me go anymore. I could be as stupid as I wanted to now—I was grown, and it was my call to make. I could stay out all night. I was no longer pressed to duck the law lest I get arrested for breaking curfew. No, all those things were behind me now. At least I was grown, even if a man I wasn't. In some ways, legal adulthood was the relief I had waited all my life for. Yet, in so many ways it was the next complication that I never expected to confront.

At that point people didn't speak as loud when you made a mistake. They allowed you your space. They would question your behavior, motives, and reasons so you could say out loud your thoughts. Then they'd quietly let you analyze your response and let you see how foolish your conclusion sounded. As youth they would spend more energy challenging your position trying to teach you the better way, but as an adult, they extended the respect of letting it be your choice to make. Imagine how many wrong answers one could come up with when one was hell-bent and determined to prove their answer and their way are right. That was the dilemma, the choice being my own, but the solutions being woefully inadequate answers to the challenges. They had all stopped speaking so loud, and in the silence, I was left to figure out the best direction all on my own. No more teachers and school administrators trying to intervene. No more mom, dad and grandparents pointing out the path of least resistance. Now, it was finally my turn to be fully in control.

I was stuck in the illusion that that place in my life was a time when it was all about me and my world. Only, the fact that I had created a child one year earlier meant that being my own man was no longer just about me but something greater than me—my son. I wish I'd gotten the memo. The one with the subject line BABY ON BOARD in big bold print. Being a young adult making mistake after mistake would not have been so bad if it had been just me who they affected. The problem was, of course, that it wasn't just me and any stupid thing I did would not only affect me, but my son as well.

I can honestly say that in my early efforts as a parent I had all the best intentions. I tried my hardest (as hard as an eighteen-year-old knows how) to live up to my ten-year-old ideal of what a good man would do for his child. The challenge was that at eighteen, life hadn't groomed me well enough to know what constituted a good man let alone a good father. I had plenty of experiences that gave me a pretty good idea of what was acceptable in terms of basic fundamentals about children; feeding, bathing, attending to them and all the daily routine of being responsible, but I had a lot to learn about the more important aspects of fatherhood. Not that any part of child rearing is any less significant than another, but the need to be just as attentive to your child's mental and emotional needs as their physiological needs is paramount. This is something that as a young parent didn't quite register in the vein of what is uncompromisingly necessary in child raising. So, while all my intentions for my child were good, a lot of times my actions and behaviors were misguided and ill applied.

By the time I learned what my grandmother meant by "the road to hell is paved with good intentions," I had made my fair share of costly mistakes. I still hadn't grasped the concept that not only was I living for me, but I needed to be living for my child, too. Still caught up in the desire for independence and right in the middle of a time period when more and more of it was being extended to me, I was blinded by the liberation of the transition. I was not clearly or fully thinking about all the implications my new-found position of leadership entailed. I was still stuck between juvenile resolves and the edge of total independence trying to balance the responsibility of a man and a father. Back then, I would have told you I was the best father there was. Looking back, I can see just how horribly wrong I really was.

It would be years of mistakes and tons of damage later before I realized how traumatic the damage I had caused was, how everything my elders said was truer than anything I could have ever formulated. Every last older member of my family could probably find any number of reasons to say "I told you so" to me. Thankfully none have. Probably because they all know me well enough to know that I'm well aware of it at this point. And, I most certainly fully understand the meaning of hindsight being 20/20.

I've made a habit of trying to analyze my every move with foresight as my first priority. However, I have lost more than I should have in terms of once-in-a-lifetime opportunities. The greatest of them all was the enormous amount of time I compromised in not being around to help my sons on their journeys to manhood.

Once you make it to the other side of a situation you can look back on it with a more objective eye and analyze it for what it really was. The greatest loss of all was exactly the thing the concerned elders in my life had spent the whole of my life trying to prevent. After living the experience, I can easily look back and see exactly what they meant. Not even the shooting incident that left me paralyzed was more costly to me than the crime I committed against my children by taking their father away from them for all these years. Not in the larger scheme of things anyway. Sure, you could argue that getting killed would have been much worse than being alive and off limits for a while, but, in reality, an absence is going to be felt just the same no matter what the cause.

That too, was a consideration for me, how I almost got myself killed and almost wasn't around to be there for my children in any capacity. Fortunately, I survived.

A little mangled and battered, but alive. Even then I couldn't recognize what I had put on the line or what was at stake. I wasn't paralyzed in a car wreck or fighting overseas in a war. I was shot because I was terrorizing someone and out of fear for his life, he shot me. He had every right to do what he did. My condition was the result of my own foolish actions. The fact that my children would have been the biggest losers if the situation had ended differently is the reality that I wasn't paying attention to. Thank God for small favors that I'm still here to write this book and for the wisdom to discern that out of very poor judgment, I have made some really bad calls.

With a more complete understanding and respect for the things of significance in my life, it's easy to see that although that incident was costly for me, the disconnect I caused by going to prison was far worse than any physical punishment ever could be. Sure, I'll be confined to a wheelchair for the rest of my life. I can live with that. I brought that on myself. The fact that my sons spent their most impressionable years without my guidance, input, love and security ranks as the most deplorable act I've ever had to own up to. That's why it's not necessary for the elders in my life to say "I told you so"—because without even trying, I understand all too well the significance of what I've done.

The very things that they had warned against out of the foresight of wisdom, my youthful stubbornness would not allow me to heed. Now many years later, all I can do is live with the guilt and pain of the mess I've created. The saddest part of the story is that my children have become victims of my immature indiscretions.

Too little, too late to change the past, but never too late to redirect the future. If we fail to use the past as a navigating tool, we will have suffered it all in vain and are prone to repeat the process. I can think of nothing more sinister than to commit a crime so costly and in the end, have gained nothing of value from it.

I told my mother one day that I hoped I lived to have half the character she and my father have. My reason for this hope was so that when the time came I could pay them back for all they had done for me, always supporting my dreams, picking me up when I fell down, believing in me when I didn't believe in myself and even carrying me at times when I should have been able to support myself. It seemed like a debt I could never repay. She told me if I wanted to fulfill my duty and make good on my debt that I would pay it forward.

Her obligation didn't end with getting me to adulthood but was unending if I could not meet the responsibility of caring for my own and equipping them to care for their own. It made sense. The proverb in the scripture that says "a wise man leaves an inheritance for his children's, children's, children" says it all. Her duties were not complete unless I was able to fulfill my own. Likewise, mine will not be complete until my own can take care of their own and so on and so on. . . This really brings into clear focus why if I allow the events of my past to have passed without giving meaning to my sons sacrifices and losses, I have not only caused their suffering, but I have done it for no meaningful gain to them at all.

What can be done to add value to a sacrifice that has been so costly? Use the wisdom learned from the lessons of the past to create a very different present. Utilize foresight to avoid the need to look back on a situation and have to examine the lesson learned in hindsight. Speak up to those going down the same road if you've lived through a troubling situation that you can help another avoid. Be a part of making things right regardless of the shame you may feel about what you have done or caused thus far. A loss is a loss, but a perpetual loss is unnecessary if you are around and able to do something about it.

This is part of the reason for me sitting down to write this book. We have gone through a situation that has cost our family an exchange for value that is highly uneven. The price you all have paid does not equal out to a good return on investment. Your childhoods were priceless and a time that you'll never be able to get back. If it took me having lived through everything I have in order to be the individual I am—I must make sure that the sacrifices you all have faced in order for me to go this road will not return to you marked bankrupt or insufficient funds. I must give meaning to your sacrifices. I must give definition to your experience. I must not let this thing transpire without capitalizing on it. I am obligated by the divine laws of creation to see to it that there is some joy born of all this pain, some good done of all this bad, some right created of so much wrong.

MANHOOD

For a man, defining manhood is probably his most daunting challenge and equally his most significant achievement. For every man the definition will be filled with a different meaning as each of us takes a very different path during our development. No two men will have the same definition of what manhood means to us. Sure, we will share some collective ideals about what it means to be a man. Our society and its norms play a huge role in shaping our shared views and beliefs about what constitutes manly behavior. Nevertheless, defining manhood is a complex and personal experience to say the least.

To highlight just how different the definition of manhood can be amongst men, I'm reminded of a story I once heard in a parenting program I helped facilitate while incarcerated. The Long Distance Dads program was a joint program with the National Fatherhood Initiative designed to help disenfranchised fathers figure out ways to stay connected and active in their children's lives. That particular day we were discussing what each participant thought made a man a man and what kinds of behavior were the defining characteristics of manhood. There were a number of good responses and a few that were less than flattering. However, none topped the example my co-facilitator shared to make a point.

He told the class about an experience that he recalled from a previous class that not only shocked his socks of, but also helped him realize how very different we all are. He said a participant was giving his feedback on manliness by giving the class an example of a phone conversation he had had some time earlier with his fifteen-year-old son. The child had gotten in trouble for joy riding in a stolen car. When the father got the son on the phone, he began to chastise the child for what he said was "the stupidest thing he could have ever done." The father asked what kind of man would catch a case for joy riding in a stolen car? His advice was, a real man would rob a bank if he was going to take a chance.

Not at all counsel I would consider appropriate, but a very clear example that each of us has internalized very different measures of what we consider constitutes real man behavior. Our determinations of what manhood is all about will largely rest on what we value as with the example of the father who gave his son the ill advice about what a real man would do if he's going to take a chance. He believed that if you were going to take a chance that could possibly land you in jail at the end, you should at least be trying to get paid in the middle. Hardly justification for giving such poor advice, but in his narrow scope of reasoning, enough.

The example, although extreme, does vividly highlight the differences in our value systems. I would hope it's safe to say that that father gave his son very bad advice. On the other hand, if you agree with what he said you will be sorely disappointed at the content of this book.

I am a firm believer that if you want to know what a man values all you have to do is pay attention to his actions. People will tell you without you asking what is important to them by each and everything they do. If a man has to keep saying he's a man but his actions dictate something else, then it's easy to discern his true character.

Life is a growing and learning process. To a large degree the man we become is based on cultural and social norms, the everyday occurrences that we view in our surroundings as normal and permissible. Most of it comes through larger media of stimuli from the world around us, like the first early lessons of the gender roles. Things like boys wear pants, are identified with the color blue, play with trucks and are expected to be rough and tumble. It is a universal norm that almost goes without saying. Nobody questions or tries to argue the opposite.

Then the scope narrows, and the medium becomes more focused on other elements like race, social-economic status, religious belief, and education level. Each element takes on its own defining characteristic in influencing the way we look at, and view, manhood. There is however an overarching message about manhood that stays consistent no matter how many of those other more narrowly placed elements influence a person's ideal. The common message to all boys about being a man is that men are supposed to be providers, protectors, leaders, and strong.

Science shows that men are more dominant than women and that element usually causes us to exhibit dominance in our activities. There is a certain amount of manhood that we automatically learn by it is constant in the world around us. One part of the strength message is delivered very early on. When a little boy falls and gets hurt in the presence of another man the message is almost always don't cry—get up and shake it off. There's an unconscious transmission of the strength ideal from one generation to the next.

How about the early messages that are conveyed from men to boys in regard to little girls or even sisters? If a four-year-old boy is playing with a little girl and a struggle begins over a toy and the boy hits the girl, he is immediately corrected with the message that boys don't hit girls. Likewise, between sisters and brothers, boys are told to look out for their little sisters and so the message that men are protectors becomes a common theme. Even little brothers of older

11

sisters will role shift in later years once they reach the stage when they believe they are strong enough to be the protector.

As we grow, other messages are constantly being reinforced over and over again, if not in our home environment, then by the other sources of input around us. To bring things into a sharper focus we can narrow the scope of influence to more specific elements like religious belief, education level, cultural norms, and national origin. Boys who are raised in homes where religion plays a big part in the family culture will receive numerous messages about a man's responsibility to his family, community, and fellow believer. They also get messages of moral correctness, virtue and charity. Boys from families with national origins of foreign lands may have strong cultural influences that drive their belief of manhood.

Likewise, Americans have a strong cultural belief in our view of manhood. This generally includes treating our counter parts as equals in the relationship structure, men acting as the heads of the family structure, and being responsible for the leadership, provision and security of the family. Given the great many different elements that are compounded to create each of our individual outlooks on manhood, it is no wonder that the growth process to manhood is filled with so many stumbling blocks and growing pains. It provides us with a better understanding of how, and why, manhood holds so much of a different meaning for all us. Although we all hold very different meanings of manhood, it's safe to say that we probably share a lot of the same ideas about positive and negative behavior. We can conclude pretty easily what negative qualities are. But what happens when the messages are conflicting? What happens when the people you look up to display behavior that is not in line with those guiding principles you learn early on?

Role Models
Being a role model is a big responsibility. This is especially true when you have thousands of admirers, as is the case of celebrities, entertainers, sports icons and the like. They may not want to be held to account for the responsibility for being a shining example, but it comes with the territory. They're not the only ones with great responsibility to be an example of positive behavior. All us who have anyone looking up to us for direction and guidance is responsible for modeling a positive image of what good character is all about.

That's the tricky part. In too many instances we men have not provided the best examples of the real character of a man. One very disappointing reality is that somewhere along the way in our era and generation irresponsibility has become fashionable behavior. This raises the question 'what do you do if the messages you receive conflict?' There is one recurring message that stands out when I think about those conflicting messages that is difficult to understand and even more difficult to correct: our approach to women and our intimate relationships.

As a young man in my social circle, sex was a ruling tenet. If you weren't getting any, you lied and said you were. If you had done it before, but weren't doing it on a regular, you lied and said you were. If neither of the above were happening—you were gay and that was final. It didn't matter if you were mentally or emotionally ready for sexual activity, you had to be getting it in or you just didn't fit. Yes, I lied between twelve and fourteen. I had to protect what little manhood I had (or thought I had anyway), but what was most important to me was making sure I got some, and quickly lest I be uncovered for the fraud I was committing.

In my little circle of influence, positive was losing your virginity as early as possible. Part peer pressure, part social glamorization—sex was very much a key element in crossing that threshold we believed to be manhood. Our music sang about it, the videos flaunted it, movies glamorized it; almost every element around us confirmed, affirmed and reiterated the value of sex in our culture, society and lives. These messages, although negative, were interpreted as positive and have not changed since.

Consequently, as a grown man, I still hear other men speaking the same language of fourteen-year-old boys. Our music has not done anything to change that mentality, nor our videos, movies, magazines or everyday male role models. The message is still convoluted, and by adulthood so reinforced in a negative respect that not only is sex, sex, sex, a firm measure of manhood, but how much, with who, and how many different chicks become the new measures of accomplishment. Sexual behavior that is supposed to be held in a covenantal and respected regard, something that is positive and very necessary in our interpersonal lives has been twisted into something destructive, immoral and debasing.

To be fair, no matter how much good parental influence is directed at the conversation, peer influence will likely trump it. The desire for a young man to fit smoothly into his peer group will likely override that good talk his mother, father or uncle had with him. The disturbing part of the equation is how many times we learn something better later and still act in the same foolish manner.

I still struggle with this challenge myself; like when I'm talking with men my age engaged in a conversation about sex and women. While they are bragging on their trophy count of women with whom they've slept, I don't raise a voice to condemn them. Instead I've found myself on too many occasions silent, or sometimes in a low voice agreeing with the speaker.

Why would I condone, even encourage a behavior I know to be inappropriate? After living on the side of believing the behavior to be appropriate, acceptable and desired, it has become a chore to act otherwise. It takes a constant effort to remember that the behavior is not correct, and a regular rebuke of that adolescent mentality to behave in a better way.

I have had to fight with the inner teen in me who still needs to feel and seem cool, manly, and macho in front of the guys. As if something about doing the right thing will compromise my masculinity. I've found it a perpetual project to reject the old negative message of sex and manhood and model a more correct and upstanding display of the significance of sex and manhood. Yet, I'm encouraged that doing so can and will be worth the sacrifice and investment.

If we are to be good role models of manhood, it will require us to relinquish those faulty perceptions we have about what manhood is all about. There were a number of faulty ideals that I held over the years that can be said to question my own feasibility as a good role model. For starters, the way I viewed masculinity. So much of my early belief of my own masculinity was wrapped up in *machismo* that not much else mattered. To be male, a man and masculine meant you had to hold your own and be able to stand on your own two feet. You had to be able to protect yourself. That meant you had to be able to fight.

There were certain expectations in boyhood that would lead to manhood, none of which included the really important characteristics, but topping the list was your ability to throw your hands. I'll never forget a conversation I had with my father about the dangers of the mean city streets in our hometown of Newark, New Jersey. I asked him what I was supposed to do if I saw trouble between me and my destination on my way home. Him, being a well-meaning academic, he said that I should turn around, go another way and take the long way home.

He had great advice. Avoid trouble and in the end protect the most valuable thing of all—yourself. The problem was that we had very different ideas of what constituted real man behavior. I thought only a coward would let a group of troublemakers deter him from getting to his destination. A real man would look trouble right in the face and go through it, even if it meant a fight was imminent as a result. His idea—exercise wisdom and avoid confrontation. My idea—make sure you show strength, dominance and force and establish your reputation, so you don't have to prove yourself a whole bunch of times. Two decades, four bullets, one wheelchair and a slew of fights later, I find that exercising wisdom is the better approach, too. Malcolm Gladwell in his book *Outliers*, explains what sociologists refer to as a "culture of honor," in an attempt to paint a picture of the reason for family feuds and violent behavior of the inhabitants of the Appalachian mountain region of Kentucky. He writes:

He's under constant threat of ruin through the loss of his animals so he has to be aggressive: he has to make clear, through his words and deeds, that he is not weak. He has to be willing to fight in response to even the slightest challenge to his reputation—and that's what a "culture of honor" means. It's a world where a man's reputation is at the center of his livelihood and self-worth.

In many ways the world I grew up in was much the same. Our community, the era, the youth—we lived in a place where predispositions were established and to live comfortably meant to fall in line. We did not create the framework for the established culture of honor that existed in our element, but it was necessity to adhere to it if we wanted to earn a place in the social structure. Fighting was not the only faulty ideal I held about masculinity. Mannerisms played a close second. The way you walked, talked, hand gestured, just about every element of your actions were being scrutinized to determine how manly you were. Passive behavior, acting with reason, being too soft spoken, having a lisp, showing feminine body language could all get you dubbed a punk, sissy, or bitch—all which could emasculate you to some level or another. This powerful microscope of scrutiny meant living up to the total predetermined perception of manhood.

That predetermined perception justified everything. Violence, breaking the law, womanizing, dishonesty, and other questionable behavior. For example, if someone criticized something about you that could be considered disrespectful it was a permission slip to go to their ass. Or, if you had committed an act that broke the law but were not caught in the act, you were mandated to maintain your silence and innocence if questioned. More times than not, the fashionable social norms through media like music and television would reinforce many of those stale and faulty dispositions. This is a phenomenon that has not gotten much better since I was a young man looking for direction. This makes it all the more difficult to redirect the attention of the following generation in a better direction. Difficult yes, impossible no.

What My Mother Said
The early inputs and influences have remained the most influential. Even though the conflicting messages of our social construct, cultural norms, peer influence,

and role models all make a very deep and lasting impression, it's the lesson of what my mother said that I resort to as an override mechanism.

It is the little things she said like "Son, a real man is responsible. He will respect women, be financially responsible, and be committed to his fellow man." I tell you, for a long time everything my mother said was in direct conflict with my outside environment. Still what my mother said has proven to be guiding principles that were never lost and are now the core of the man I am today.

What My Father Said

My mother and father spoke much the same language when it came to qualities, characteristics and responsibilities of a man, albeit in very different words. The message at the end of the day was pretty consistent. Being that my father was an academic, his focal points and conversations on the defining features of manhood consisted of one main theme—think. He said and did a lot of things that I believe were instrumental in helping me grow into a well-rounded adult, but the one that sticks out the most vividly is his conversation about the importance and art of critical thinking. This is a skill he honed throughout his many years as an educator, and one that has proved to be invaluable in my own life. I remember thinking as a kid that God had cursed me for allowing me to be the son of a man who chose teaching as a profession. It was hell being the son of a college professor. But years later I'm glad that my life has afforded me that experience.

I can't begin to list all the great lessons my parents gave me. A lifetime of work and dedication is too much to try to squeeze into the pages of this or any other book. Besides, it is a contribution that is continuously evolving as each of us grows into different stages of our own lives and experiences. But the entirety of the content that lies between these pages is exactly that—a glimpse at the great lessons my parents shared, the ones I learned on my own, and those I learned by other means.

The men we are, who we will become are collective compositions of all the elements that have influence in our lives. We will pick and choose certain qualities and attributes that we find desirable from all sorts of people over a lifetime. It is the thing about us that makes us unique and special. Each of us is his own different man, but there are a number of individual qualities that we can and should internalize and view with some level of significance. The rest of this message speaks to those individual building blocks.

16

CHARACTER

Character is the element that truly defines a man. It is based on your values, which in turn are deeply rooted in your morals and beliefs. Character is a measuring stick. Character cannot be taught. Because it is a combination of a number of other qualities, it is impossible to teach character alone. Instead, it has to be continually impressed upon an individual over a period of time. The best lessons of character are more often than not modeled. In instances when it is directly referred to, it is usually done so by saying what is inappropriate character behavior.

The reason for this is that character can only be determined by watching someone's behavior. Hence the reason it's most often taught by modeling good examples of it, and why it's most often referred to when inappropriate behavior is being displayed. The one feature of character that makes it difficult to identify and gauge is that it is an internal function which requires us to be introspective in its analysis. Character is a developmental feature that happens gradually over time, is years in the making and one of the more difficult elements for us to bring into awareness and cultivation.

Nonetheless, it is a part of us that we must recognize, attend to, nurture, and develop if we are to be the best men we can possibly be. Your character will define you to others. It will be a signature of that which you value the most. If you lack character depth, it will not only show but it will likely cause you a great deal of hardship during the course of your life.

A lot of your success will depend on your ability to demonstrate good character qualities. People are more willing and desirous of dealing with those they believe to be good natured. In so many ways, your whole reputation is wrapped up in the depth of your character. My father used to tell me all the time that looks can only get you so far. He said it to drive home his critical thinking point, of course. He would always finish with "you've got to have something of value between those ears." Closing with "you can only look at a pretty, stupid person for so long." I later changed his philosophy to give a similar message but a whole different meaning. I'd say, "good looks will only get you so far; if you lack character, people will see through you and you won't make it far in a world where we need one another to make things happen." That was my message to my kids, and sometimes a friend or family member who may have been in need of hearing it. Sure, I mentioned the intellect part, but the center of my conversation was mostly based on character.

Character building is an intimate process that requires some level of realness. You have to be able to critically and objectively do self-assessments in order to find the place where true character building can happen. You will not notice your own character flaws until someone else points them out to you. It is not a comfortable experience to have someone pointing out your flaws. Human nature is to jump on the defensive and try to justify your behavior. Most people will avoid acknowledging their flaws, never mind trying to identify with them and attempting to improve it. So, in making an effort to approach character building with any remote chances of success, you will have to practice stable behavior.

In order to measure areas of your character that may be less than desirable, you have to have a consistent behavior to measure against. That way you can hear the message clearly as it's being delivered to you. I have struggled with the one character defect that I consistently attempt to improve—being argumentative. I like consistency. Therefore, I find it easy to keep my behavior the same most of the time, even when the trait is less than desirable. But when you hear a consistent message about something you're doing, it might be time to listen to the messenger and take the hint.

In my case, the message was "you just won't stop. You've got to have the last word. And you can't admit when you're wrong." Of course, I didn't feel like what people were saying was exactly correct, but I can't deny that the message was consistent across the board. I finally got the point when I had matured enough to critically evaluate what people had been saying with objective eyes. After all, everyone couldn't be saying the same thing about me and all be wrong. At some point, I had to consider that all these non-related people had to be speaking some truth.

That's the thing about character, if you are not used to being critical and analytical about yourself it will be hard to hear the need for improvement from outside sources as they come. Defining your character is intimate, but interpersonal too. The defining elements of who you are and what you represent will only be on display in your interpersonal affairs. If a person does not show proper consideration for his elders, or an older sibling, proper care for a younger, it is easy to determine that their character leaves something to be desired. Likewise, the individual who shows considerable respect for the wisdom of age, and care for the inability of youth, is determined to be a person of distinction.

Character is the sum total of the traits that define you. Individual qualities that are essential in making us all distinguished men. It is things like strength, creativity, honesty and integrity (good character), or dishonesty, laziness and greed (bad character). It is what we should use to measure each other. It is the element that

18

will dictate our behavior, and a part of us that we cannot afford to ignore. It is the one element in us that should always be at the forefront of our minds and atop the priority list for things in our lives we choose to cultivate. Just as growth, maturation and development are lifelong efforts, character building is too.

IDENTITY

Who are you? So much is wrapped up in identity. The element or thing that we most identify with. Identity is the answer to the question "who am I?" Identifying yourself should be an easy process. It's about standing out and being distinctly known and recognized as something in particular. The only challenge, for people—identifying is about association. Even the formal definition of identity is as complex as a people's quest to define themselves. In as much as identity means individuality and distinction, it also means collective characteristics that associate an individual with group (in terms of identifying with something).

To be perfectly honest, I'm only just now coming to some place of consistency in my own identity. It has taken such a long time because of the mixed messages that I have experienced over time. Blacks in America have not been afforded the privilege of being able to trace their origins. That disconnect has left us in the precarious place of not having a foundation to associate with. While most other nationalities have a clear and exact knowledge of where their family roots are, we have not been so fortunate. For most of us, there is a burning desire to know where we came from. The condition of not knowing cannot be much help in helping us find that place of comfort in establishing our identity.

I can't speak for all, but I can say that the lack of a definitive cultural origin has caused a bit of confusion in my own life. If we were Oriental, we could identify with Asian customs. Middle Eastern, European or Latino, they all have distinct customs that identify them as one distinct element. The Black American has been created. We are the amalgamation of numerous different European cultures and numerous different African nations about which we know very little. Even that connection with our lineage is artificial. We have borrowed as we became liberated; little bits and pieces of African culture, customs, names and lifestyles trying to piece back together some semblance of an identity. These are mostly vain attempts to find an area of comfort and belonging.

At some point I learned to accept that my origins were in Africa, Europe, America, and maybe some other places as well. History has told me that there are many different nations of blood coursing through my veins. Still it's no consolation for the desire to know my beginning. I don't even think that my biggest source of confusion was a lack of origin in the beginning. I think it was what the world was telling me about myself. As a young man, it was the world view that created the most confusing message of all.

Becoming aware of the aforementioned realizations about race and origin was not the biggest or most relevant factor in my attempt to define myself. It took some level of awareness, knowledge of the past, and a whole lot of reality checks to draw such a complex conclusion. The most, significant mixed message about my identity was the one I had bombarding my space daily in the early years.

I am a hip-hop baby. It was born when I was born, and like twins we have grown up together. The music was an intimate part of creating a culture that was very influential. The songs described the elements I saw around me, and the images were so closely related to things I was familiar with it was unreal. It was easy to identify with, and even easier to latch on to. There were messages in the music that told the story of my everyday life.

Being a little boy in the urban inner city was like being the main character in the songs those groups were making. Songs about police brutality, distrust of the law, gangs, and the dangers of street life all seemed to echo the movie of my life. They gave a voice to my reality. Music wasn't the only factor in establishing my identity. My father had a huge impact on shaping it as well. His message was always in conflict with what I believed was important as a young man. Just as I could not understand the rationale or importance in avoiding the trouble of a fight, I couldn't understand much of his other rationale either.

I didn't understand his advice to submit to a system that had abused us in the past. Especially since the way I was seeing it, it was still mistreating us at the time. He advised that law enforcement officials were there to help us. From what I saw they did more harassing than helping. He advised that we needed to get a good education because education was the only ticket to success. I saw a substandard school system underserving its students. He said that I should be removed from the elements of our community (people and their activities) because it was trash and of little value if I wanted to be somebody and go somewhere. I saw my friends, men and women, young and old, that looked just like me. He advised a lot of things that at the time I could not understand. The more he implored me to do one thing, the more I did the exact opposite.

I didn't understand social status. Reputation, association and distinction did not quite fit into my schema, and no amount of counsel or advice was helping me get it. As an adult I can fully recognize and appreciate my father's wise words. I'm no longer disillusioned by the belief that his rejection of certain elements that didn't measure up to appropriate standards of manhood was somehow a rejection of me. I'll never forget the time when we were on a car ride and he told me, "I don't want you to end up like this trash" referring to our neighbors. I was almost in

21

tears as I tried to wrap my mind around what he meant. I saw the people in our community as my people. His rebuke of them, in my young mind, was a rejection of me.

The community was all I had. My school, friends, relatives and the neighborhood were my world. I could not separate myself from it. There was a very real message beginning to be conveyed. Whether in school, in our neighborhood or elsewhere I was coming into a real knowledge of what part race plays in America. As a man I can hear clearly the message my father delivered in those early years. His encouragement that black meant having to prove yourself twice as much. Working three times as hard. Submit to the authority that has what you want and take whatever crap you must to get what and where you need to be. These were all messages that would be guiding forces that would later help me navigate through the choppy waters of maturation.

As a youngster I wanted to believe in his ideas. However, the reality of what was happening around me was a forceful contradiction. Like the time when my godbrother and I got profiled and targeted by detectives because we fit the description of some car thieves. I was fifteen at the time. It was Friday night, and my father was on his way out to New York to party. As he dressed, he asked me to go to the ATM for him and get a few bucks. I got his card and my godbrother, and I walked a block and a half to the ATM to withdraw the money. As we stood at the machine, I noticed an old model Oldsmobile driving past us slowly and the driver and passenger eyeing us extremely hard.

We got the money (about $140) and, as we walked through the small park leading back to the street we lived on, I noticed the same car creeping slowly back up the street towards us. One thing about streetwise kids is they have an uncanny ability to detect when something isn't right. Assuming the occupants of the car who had just seen us at the ATM were going to try to rob us, I told my godbrother if they turned down our street to run. Sure enough, the car turned down our street and slowed to a rolling stop about fifty feet away from us. I looked back, and the passenger had emerged from the car clutching a semiautomatic handgun and headed right towards us.

I yelled "break," and headed back in the direction we had come from. I was only a few feet away from a busy street and on instinct I darted out in traffic because I knew the car couldn't make a U-turn and catch me. Nor, could the one gunman chase two people. My godbrother wasn't so lucky. He slipped on one of those metal doors on the sidewalk that are service inlets to buildings on city streets. When he caught his footing and was able to run, the gunman was about fifteen feet from him blocking him from running the same way I had gone.

I quickly dipped into a city subway station and called my dad from a pay phone. I explained what had just happened as best I could between gasping for air and trying to keep my voice down in case my assailant was still in pursuit. I stayed put until my dad arrived and I tried my best to tell him what had happened through the excitement and nervous energy still stirring inside me. He listened. Then, we set out to find out what happened to my god-brother (his godson) who I believed might have been dead.

Downtown Newark has a lot of one-way streets. As luck would have it, on the drive home, we circled a couple of blocks and ran right into my godbrother. The police had him palms flat on the front of a police car, putting one hand behind his back getting cuffed. I pointed him out to my dad, and he parked the car to go investigate what was going on. I was totally lost as to how he went from running from an armed robber to getting arrested inside of twenty minutes, but the answer was soon forthcoming.

The scene had several police cars, two unmarked and three or so uniformed squad cars. There was a badly wrecked vehicle, an ambulance, and a young man sitting in the back of one of the police cars in handcuffs. My father approached the arresting officer who was seconds away from putting my godbrother in the back of one of the empty squad cars to ask what was going on and why they were arresting his godson. The officer told him that he (my godbrother) was identified as the driver of a stolen car that had caused the accident that we saw getting cleaned up in front of us. He concluded by saying that the young man they already had in custody had confirmed that my godbrother was the driver.

The accident had been a bad one. The driver hit another car causing it to hit a city bus. One person was rushed to the hospital in critical condition and two others had minor injuries. My father heard him out, then rebuffed this version of the facts. My father, who was also a part-time correctional officer, produced his badge, and began explaining how that couldn't be the case because his godson and myself had just been with him roughly thirty minutes earlier. That in fact, we were on an errand for him to get some money from the ATM and promptly return home to the apartment on the very street where the detectives jumped out on us.

All those things were confirmation enough to convince the officer of my godbrother's innocence. He released the cuffs from his wrist and turned him over to my dad's custody. They came back to the car and my godbrother settled into the back seat doctoring a busted lip. He filled me in on what happened after we got split up on our mad getaway. He was chased down the block just past my father's apartment when his assailant, a cop, finally shouted "stop running!

Police!" At which time I would imagine a sense of relief came over him, seeing as how we initially thought they were robbers; right up until the officer punched him in the mouth for making him chase him down.

Can you believe the injustice? Or my indignation at the perceived injustice anyway. We were just two young kids doing what our parent had requested. We happened to fit-the-description, in the right place at the wrong time. I was livid at the thought. These were our public servants whose job it was to protect and serve (that included us too, I thought) and there they were abusing and mistreating us for something we didn't do. I passionately rallied for my dad to go back and do something; file a complaint, beat them up, anything to let them know that they couldn't just go around abusing innocent kids like that. I sat in the passenger seat yet again, almost in tears listening to my father as he told me that "what we're going to do was go home and be grateful that we got him before it got any worse."

He gave us a speech about knowing when to submit and who to challenge and when. He said, "there are forces out there that you don't try to go against." His conversation felt like betrayal in that moment. If we couldn't count on our parents to fight for us, who could we count on? It was those messages that caused the greatest confusion about who I was, where I belonged, and how I could make it through this labyrinth of challenges I would soon face.

My father was right to address his concern for our well-being in a blunt force trauma way. The cops didn't roll up on us badges out—but guns drawn. Their clothes did not hint law enforcement officials. Their car did not scream authority. Instead, all those elements were masked. We were reading the nonverbals— which all screamed DANGER and TROUBLE. My dad knew those dangers all too well. Names like Oscar Grant and the Fruitvale Station killing, when a police officer shot a handcuffed black man while he lay helplessly face down on a train station platform getting arrested; Sean Bell, shot numerous times at his bachelor party the day before his wedding in New York; Amadou Diallo, the 22-year-old African immigrant killed in a hail of NYPD bullets as he reached for his wallet; Jonathan Ferrell, the 24-year-old FAMU graduate, shot dead in Charlotte, North Carolina by police after he went looking for help after getting into a car accident; or Michael Brown, the 18-year-old unarmed teen shot six times by police as he held his hands up in Ferguson, Missouri. All examples of what could have happened that night we got chased. Looking back, I guess a busted lip and bruised pride wasn't so bad after all.

It was the conversation with my dad about how to use the system to get what you want and ahead in life that was at odds with my relative reality. It was that very

24

system that was seemingly not going to give me and others like me an easy or fair shake. After all, if all it took to be a target of the very establishment that we were supposed to respect, trust, and submit to was to fit the description, it was going to be a hard row to hoe in being trusting, receptive and open to much else. Profiling, stereotyping and categorizing were hardly words in my vocabulary yet, much less concepts in my mind. Those are elements that would have to be learned in time, after a certain amount of awareness had been obtained.

Still, no matter how unprepared we are, we will be faced with those or similar realities. We have to choose who we will be, how we will be identified, associated and ultimately defined. I had to choose what was comfortable for me, as we all have had to do at one point or another. In the earlier years it's a constant search for validation and esteem from all areas in our lives.

At first, we aim to please our parents. Soon after, the esteem of our peers becomes a priority. Later on, social acceptance in different social structures like college fraternities, organizations in the community, or our church. At some point, when we feel accomplished in those areas, we'll seek the validation that our life and contribution have made a difference. This is the time in life when we self-actualize and find fulfillment in caring and doing for others, provided we get to that level of consciousness.

Before I could verbalize the steps in establishing an identity, I had to learn to differentiate between those two very distinct realities I was presented. There is a fine line that distinguishes one from the other. Walking that line is a delicate process that takes some level of skill that is hard to teach. The world of comfort (the stereotypical thug appeal) was two worlds away from the world of necessity (institutional conformance). I felt like if I gave in to a system/establishment that was prone to treating me with contempt like a criminal or worse, I was somehow compromising myself. Of course, I had no idea who I was and even less of an idea of who I should be aiming to become.

I, like many other young men in my position, was seeking acceptance in the element that most resembled me, my experience, the things I believed to be important, the people, places and things that were a constant in my environment. It's hard to see when you are caught in the middle of things the profoundness in elementary sayings like "birds of a feather flock together," and "you are only as good as the company you keep." It's an even greater challenge to conceptualize just how off course you really are when you are seeking esteem, validation, camaraderie, community, and the feeling that association provides, especially when the traditional/mainstream social construct is not the most inviting or receptive to the element you choose to embrace.

25

There is no easy answer to the identity conundrum for young men (black males especially). You can spend a lifetime adhering to the mainstream school of thought climbing the establishment ladder of success and still be met with challenges like that of black Harvard Professor, Henry Gates. Dr. Gates was arrested by the Cambridge Police for trying to get into his own home. Dr. Gates is a historian, scholar and the Director of the W.E.B DuBois Institute for African and African American Research among other things, who in spite of his numerous achievements is still challenged with disproving suspicion simply because of his race. It is a clear and resolute example of the difficulty of conveying the message that my father was trying to express that day so many years ago in the car, one of the continuous lessons in his "you will have to be smarter, work harder, fold 'em at the right time, and stand up when you have to" message. The most important message was to develop the ability to think rationally and critically and have the ability to know when to do what.

Sociology Professor, Elijah Anderson of Yale University wrote in his book *Code of the Streets: Decency, Violence, and Moral Life in the Inner City*; about a condition known as 'code shifting.' Central to the thesis of his book was the fact that black men have an extra element of assimilation to overcome. In many instances, young men will have to shift their code of conduct numerous times in a day in order to successfully engage the simplest activities. Three very distinct codes that stand out from his book were those of: 1) The need to match his peers on his home turf. In instances where children come from low income or impoverished neighborhoods, this may entail playing the 'thug roll' in order not to be a target. 2) The need not to be perceived as a threat, in school, at the mall or commercial shopping districts, and especially in the eyes of law enforcement officials [after all, they have a license to kill]. 3) In everyday encounters with people of other races (especially white people).

Professor Anderson explains that many times white America cannot differentiate between decent young black men and those considered troublemakers. To the white majority, all young black men are perceived as aggressive and dangerous until they prove otherwise. Trayvon Martin was a vivid example of the prejudice and contempt that still exists to this day for young black men in America. During the George Zimmerman trial, we heard numerous instances where Zimmerman made assumptions, negative statements, and presumptive conclusions that ultimately lead to him killing the youth because in his mind, "he fit the description."

Association is important. Not only will it identify the good in you, but it can also brand you as something you don't want to be thought of or known as. It is an unfortunate fact of life that we will be identified by stereotypes that will place us in very narrow categories. It doesn't leave us much room to display our character depth, and if you think about it, there may just be a small amount of validity to that train of thought. After all, if it walks like a duck, quacks like a duck, and acts like a duck—then it's probably a duck. On many occasions, young black men will be crossed with the task of disproving skepticism, apprehension and a bit of hostility just based on their race. The prejudice that accompanies this type of behavior can prompt a whole new set of dangers. But for the fact that Jordan Davis and his friends liked loud rap music--he might still be alive.

We criticize any faction that profiles, stereotypes and categorizes and passes judgment too quickly, but the truth is that we all do it. It's the practice of character assessment. That's why it's so important to pay close attention to what it is we are saying by the things we don't say, by the way we dress, the way we speak, the company we keep, and the activities we engage in. There is a nonverbal conversation that goes on between people at all times. Our identity is the first words we speak to people about us. Depending on what you are saying in that nonverbal encounter, you will be well or poorly perceived and received. It is the first impression that is so vital to how the world will interact with you. Jordan Davis, the young man who was shot to death by an angry older white man was a good kid, from a good home. His killer didn't agree with his choice of music. He could not see beyond the pounding images, the black faces and the loud music invoked in his mind. That young man did not deserve to die like he did. However, he did not code shift that day in time enough to save his life.

It is important to establish an identity that is comfortable, but more importantly, one that is healthy, balanced and complete. That is not always the easiest thing to do in an environment that may not be hospitable to black men, foreigners, the unusual, the alternative or any other element that is perceived as out of the norm, but it is a must if we are to become completely balanced and well-rounded men. In some instances, it may even save your life.

As men, it is our responsibility to set examples for boys so they can fashion their own identity in solid characteristics that will serve them well throughout a lifetime. There are, unfortunately, more than enough poor examples of manhood out there for them to identify with. There are enough bad boy sports figures, rappers and entertainers to set two centuries of poor examples to shape their identities. Our job is the same as my father's was in trying to get me to understand the things I couldn't; the challenge of defining that fine line between the two worlds of comfort and necessity.

In all fairness, some lessons will take a longer time to conclude. They will be hard fought at times, at the expense of many hurt feelings and sometimes (like in the case of my godbrother) a little blood and some physical pain. However, it's our task to impart those vital messages and provide close proximity examples of true manhood for young men to identify with. We can ease the burden of finding one's self by what we provide.

PRIDE

Pride is an awesome thing when it is put into proper context. It is equally an element that could be the cause of a lot of unnecessary suffering if it is left unchecked and unabated. Pride can be an element of strength, distinction, definition and huge value in helping us navigate through life. When we have a sense of pride we carry an element that acts as a bonding agent in the sense that we are able to remain put together even under circumstances that test us. Pride is something we are taught very early in life. Race pride, nation pride, self-pride, pride in your family, your religious community, school, job, company—you name it, we claim it. A strong sense of pride is very American if it's nothing else.

Given the importance of pride in establishing our identity and creating the character we desire it is important to examine the elements of pride that can cause us harm or setbacks before celebrating the dynamics of pride that are truly the defining, and meaningful measures.

Foolish Pride
This is the kind the elders warn against; pride that doesn't know that it is being or behaving in a manner that is unbecoming. Foolish pride is what will cause a man not to ask for help when it is evident that he needs it, like when you're driving in a car in an unknown area, you're lost, and you refuse to ask for directions. Thank God we have GPS for that particular illness of foolish pride. But what about the kind of foolish pride that no amount of GPS treatment can cure? Like the kind of foolish pride that takes place when we are suffering from some other illness like alcoholism, drug addiction, or some other type of self-destructive behavior? What happens when we allow our pride to get between us and treatment for our illness?

Those are the times when pride can lead to self-destruction. If not that extreme, consider the toll it takes on our families and loved ones. Self-destructive behavior has adverse effects not only on us, but also on all those around us, our immediate and extended family, our co-workers, and the community. When we don't perform at our best, we rob all those we are connected to.

We get into unhealthy habits that will carry over into every aspect of our lives. Foolish pride is unhealthy pride. Unhealthy pride is the kind that says, "I'm too proud to beg." Would you beg if your life depended on it? Maybe the answer is no, but think about it; if you died, who would you be hurting? Certainly not yourself, death alleviates all physical pain. Are we selfish enough to believe our pride is worth dying over? There are not many things I could think of are worth dying for. Yet, I have seen too many occasions when pride has caused a person to lose his life over a corner, an article of clothing, some other material or immaterial thing—even the color of a shirt. These are all things that seem legitimate sources of pride until you take in the bigger picture and assess how truly infantile they really are.

There is a Chinese story about a master martial arts teacher that expresses the example of how to exercise true and real pride. There was a master martial arts teacher walking alone on a quiet country road headed from one village to another. On his way he was stopped by a band of four gang members who would beat and rob passersby on their journeys. The gang leader told the Master to "state your business." The old man replied, "I'm trying to get to the next village just beyond the ridge."

The gang leader laughed telling the old man "the only way you can get through is to get on your knees and crawl through my legs or we will beat you." The old man didn't respond. The gang leader taunted him and repeated. "The only way to pass this point is through my legs or we will beat you."

The old man walked close to the young man, fell to his knees and crawled through his legs and continued his journey. As he walked away, he could hear the young men laughing amongst themselves talking about how cowardly the old man had behaved in doing what he did.

The old man made it to his destination. Sometime later when word had gotten around the village that the young thugs had belittled the Master that way, a young village boy asked the Master why he didn't just fight the thugs. Surely, he could have killed them all without even trying. The old man replied, "they did not know who I was."

There is so much wisdom in his simple statement, but the highlight is that he was not moved by his pride. Instead he acted in wisdom realizing these young men who did not know better were being governed by a foolish and unhealthy pride that he had long since outgrown. It is that kind of pride that can and will serve us best once we are able to master the ability to be poised in pride so that we can act in the wisdom of the old Master and not the foolishness of the young thugs.

Real Pride
Real pride is quiet, like the Master who could have announced his identity. Instead of loudly promoting his advanced fighting ability, he showed them internal

and mental strength. He submitted to degrading conditions in order to preserve the important thing—life.

Real pride takes a level of humility and grace that is not available to the mentally and emotionally weak. Imagine the ridicule that will accompany the belief by others that you are weak. In a society where the culture of its men is to show strength, dominance and power at all times, the perception that you are weak in any way will be a direct attack on your self-esteem. The idea that any man can look those odds in the eyes with a willingness to accept all that comes with it has a strength in pride that stands alone.

Balance
The greatest challenge with pride is finding that medium, the pivot point that helps you keep from being that fool who is too proud to beg for your life when something like drugs or alcohol threatens to steal it, the pride that is that center point of gravity that is equal to the magnetic poles that guide and pull the needle on the compass in a singular direction, that which helps keep us grounded and going in the right direction as we journey through this growth process called life.

In order to establish and maintain healthy pride about ourselves, we have to use the following words in the context of pride so that we are well situated on the true definition of pride: graciousness, quietness, humbleness, strength, poise, and balance. If we keep those words at the forefront of our thinking when we look to define pride, we will certainly have a well-rounded definition of what pride looks like.

The pride message will be conferred to our young men through a number of media and sources. It is our duty to make completely certain that the entirety of the message comes through loud and clear. Where life does not provide us with experiences like the one of the Master and the thugs, we must be sure to impress the importance of the story's true moral message and meaning.

Healthy pride is a critical element in shaping boys into healthy, balanced and well-rounded men. It is not only a shame not to convey the proper message about pride from our men to boys, it's a crime as well. Failure to pass along the proper message and meaning of pride is to rob a young man of a character trait that he will undoubtedly need. To be proud of yourself—who you are—is a jewel of self-esteem that will be an absolute in times when the messages from the world are contradictory.

DIGNITY

Dignity is another uncompromising element and characteristic that, like pride, is essential. Like pride, it is a silent element of character that will help you through tough times and circumstances. However, dignity, unlike pride, lacks a downside. Pride is an element that must be checked and balanced. Dignity, on the other hand, is a characteristic that can never be in over abundance. It's something that is rarely taught by name but built over time as an outgrowth of instilling well-balanced pride.

Dignity is a sense of esteem. It is what we feel when we perceive ourselves as valuable. The dictionary defines it thus: 1) "The quality or condition of being esteemed honored, or worthy, 2) Self-esteem and poise." I particularly like the idea of self-esteem and poise. Poise is balance, stability, and assurance. The pairing of self-esteem and poise is essentially to say one is self-confident in their self-worth in a balanced, stable and self-assured way.

What lesson or lessons do we go through that teaches us the meaning and value of dignity? Each person will have a different answer to this question but will likely share one thing in common: no singular lesson is a defining measure.

The Uncompromising
As we grow, develop, and mature, we encounter situations that test our character. At these critical junctions, the nature of who we really are will surface and our values will shine through. That is how we are able to measure just how dignified we truly are. Because one person's idea of what is dignified may not be the same as another's, it is wise to focus on the general tenor of the value of being dignified and behaving in a dignified way. For those of us who exhibit dignified behavior habits, we produce a stabilizing feature that makes it difficult for others to treat us otherwise.

Provided you know the meaning of dignity and have some level of values that define it to, and for you, you should make it an "uncompromisable" element. Because your dignity is a testament to how you think and feel about yourself, it is paramount that you not compromise it for anyone or anything. Not a lover, money, material things, or social positioning. The world, or people, will reflect back to you what you put out. If you lack self-esteem, balance, stability, and assurance, it will be impossible to expect or request that others treat you as if you have them. The best and only way to be considered as worthy of the esteems of others is to project it yourself first.

Remaining Dignified Through Undignified Situations

If you live long enough and haven't already experienced a situation that puts you in an undignified position, you will. It is an unpleasant fact of life that no matter how you perceive and carry yourself, there will be people who will not show you the respect and dignity that you deserve. It's unfortunate and unpleasant, but this is a reality that we must learn to deal with, maneuver through and come out on top of.

In those times, it takes a strong sense of self-love and worth to retain the element of dignity that is essential to harmonious balance. One example of this that comes to mind is the many times during my incarceration that I was strip-searched. It was a process that as an inmate I was subjected to at any time, for any reason. At times, it was procedural, like coming back from visitation, going on an outside doctor's trip, or being transferred from one location to another. At any given moment, it could also be done for suspicion of wrong-doing as well.

I was fortunate in that most of the ones I did endure were procedural and simply the price one had to pay to visit with family, check one's health, or move to the next location, which meant advancing through the process and getting closer to home. Nonetheless, each time was a test of my ability to remain dignified under difficult circumstances. After spending a lifetime undressing only in privacy and comfort, where and when I wanted to, it was an unpleasant experience to have to disrobe when told to, in front of people that I would have to see every day for years to come. Sure, it was all a part of the experience that's geared towards punishment and to a lesser extent "correction" of bad behavior. The reality was, however, just another of many dehumanizing elements that caused each man to dig deep to preserve and reserve his own dignity.

That is an extreme example of a situation that causes undignified circumstances. You may never be faced with such a grave challenge, but if you live long enough, some challenge will arise. It can be as simple as someone spreading vicious rumors about you, or as complex as being blamed for theft. No matter what the scenario, the feeling will be the same—unpleasant, disconcerting and painful. You will have to remind yourself that you are more than your current condition, defined by your circumstances, and that what is happening is temporary, that what you are enduring only has the power over you that you give it. Your dignity is not something anyone can take from you. In every instance that you allow your dignity to be compromised or taken, you have given it away.

Retention Through Degradation

Retaining dignity through degradation is tough. It is similar to remaining dignified in undignified situations, but it is harder. As with the example of the strip search,

33

those conditions were the result of the rules of the administrative establishment, a side effect of the condition. No one sought out to put anyone in a situation that was challenging to their dignity. It was an effect that transpired by default. It was just the result of how we are groomed, to be private about our unclothed bodies that made it feel like an undignified situation. Similarly, if your dignity is put into a questionable position because of some external factors like gossip or accusations, there may not be any intent to attack and hurt you.

The same is not true of degradation. When something is done to degrade someone, it is usually done purposefully, spitefully and with malicious intent. That means it's more painful, more challenging to withstand, and definitely more challenging to overcome. To be degraded means that your adversary is seeking to rob you of the very elements that dignity is comprised of. There is no honor, esteem, or worthiness in degradation. It consists of humiliation, debasement, and a distinct measure of worthlessness. To overcome that takes a little more than a strong sense of self-worth.

It takes a strong mental will to retain dignity through situations and circumstances of degradation. Balance, stability and assurance are impossible goals for the individual who does not have the mental capacity to stay grounded in extreme circumstances where degradation is their nemesis. Dignity is an internal element that is rarely spoken of and always silently guarded by its keeper as a personal treasure. To remain dignified through a degrading situation will require you to draw from both your mental strength and internal treasure chest of values to harness the power necessary to remain dignified under any circumstances.

The Importance
The value of dignity should be self-explanatory. If there is any question as to its importance, just consider what life would look like without it. It is a stabilizing component. It helps all us to be able to find balance when none exists, to be reassured in times when things look uncertain, stable when life throws fast-balls at us and everything seems topsy-turvy and out of focus. It allows us the self-confidence we need to present ourselves in an honorable and proud manner that will command esteem and speak volumes of our self-worth and consequently, our value to others. There is no question that the value of dignity is priceless.

It is one of many things that should be shown in your actions. It is not something that you have to advertise in a loud voice. If you have it, it will show in the way you carry yourself. It is the kind of thing that once you master it, you will never have cause to question your self-worth. The world can throw all kinds of challenges your way. With dignity, you can survive them with poise and assurance that you are worthy of respect and honor.

Honor

The Value

The value of honor is another element that will serve us well. It is another valuable character trait that separates the average from the extraordinary. It too, is silent, internal, and like so many other things about character, takes other people and situations to examine and measure. It is a characteristic that is instilled over the course of time and can be seen when we are forced into situations that challenge it.

A promise to a friend, the vows we exchange at marriage, an agreement with a business partner, taking a job as a civil servant—these are all situations that require honor to fulfill. Any and all agreements we make are hinged on our ability to honor what we agree to. The vow spouses make is an agreement to honor the sanctity of the marriage bond. The agreement of a judge, doctor, law enforcement officer or service member is an agreement with the community and society to protect, serve and not misappropriate or abuse their power. They should honor the responsibility that is conferred with their position and serve the public to the best of their ability.

Honor should remain a constant goal in all our doings. We live in a world where winning is essential to survival. Sometimes winning can cause people to compromise their values in order to accomplish a goal. For the man who makes being honorable a constant goal, there will be fewer instances of succumbing to dishonorable ways in order to achieve his goals. It is unrealistic to think that a man will always do the honorable thing. There are many instances when a man may act in a manner that is dishonorable and undignified and may not realize his error. It is not a crime to fall short of upstanding character. The crime is perpetrated when a man acts dishonorable and learns nothing from it.

Remaining Honorable When Others Don't

As men, we are responsible only for our own actions. It's easy to shift our responsibility for our own behavior to the cause and effect of external circumstances and conditions. It is an all-too-common occurrence to see a man blame his actions/reactions on the actions of others. I remember a man I would converse with who would say and do contradictory things. He was in his fifties and considered himself a conscious individual. He would comment to me that it bothered him to see two grown men standing three feet from each other and shout at one another while having a conversation.

I fully understood his frustration. It was bothersome to me, too. The day came when I saw the guy and another individual engaged in a spirited debate. The unusual thing about this discussion was that the man I would talk to regularly was shouting at the other gentlemen in the very manner he had been so critical of in others. After their conversation concluded, I pulled the guy up and questioned his behavior. After all, he had been very vocal and critical about his disdain for that kind of carrying on. In a heated haste he said, "that man made me raise my voice. It's the only way he could understand me."

His reply wasn't surprising. In fact, it was typical of any individual seeking to minimize their wrongdoing. The point is that we cannot afford to blame our faulty behavior on what other people do or don't do. The same is true in upholding our honor. There will be times when others will totally lack even the semblance of honor. More times than you'll care to have to deal with in fact. That is no excuse to compromise yours. It is a time for you to stand even firmer on your own. That does not mean that you continuously engage a person that you come to realize lacks honor in their character. In fact, it should act as a gauge that you use to determine the fitness of that individual to continue in your intimate space.

Separation
If you find that a person lacks honor, it is a perfect time and excuse to separate yourself from them. First, their actions will be disrespectful to your person and disorienting to your own efforts. Second, you will be associated and thought of in the same vein as them by others. Yes, it goes right back to the identity tenet. It's hard to imagine or see things as different when they are closely related. Picture a preacher in a strip club or a straight-laced, non-drug user in a crack house. They don't fit. Third, bad habits are corrosive. You can only stand so much of anything before it starts to wear of on you. It is always a best practice to observe an individual's behavior and "be ye removed" if it does not line up with your values, morals, and beliefs.

Honor in the Un-honorable
Is there honor in the un-honorable? The answer is not as simple as the question would have you to believe. It can be said that any behavior that by majority consensus is dishonorable could never be honorable, but I'd implore you to think critically here. I consider murder barbarism. Society sanctions murder by going to war. Then they celebrate the murderers who survive the carnage with medals of honor and honorable discharges from the service. I value human life and consider killing sinful and wrong no matter who's doing it or how it's done. The war-mongers who beat the war drum to rally public support would have you believe it's a necessary evil. They promote it with slogans like "A few good men,"

36

and "The few, the finest, the Marines," painting a picture that screams honor in no uncertain terms. Murder is murder. A killer is a killer, and both are disgraceful and dishonorable be they the United States Armed Forces, or Boko Haram, ISIS, Al Qaeda or the FARC.

It is an oxymoron that is not easily explained. It is not a stand-alone scenario either. You may find that life will present you with a great many situations that you believe to be honorable that another may believe to be dishonorable. You will have to judge if the impending circumstances are worthy of the action necessary to meet the need. The most important factor in any case where you have to determine the honorableness of your action is to choose and stand firm in your conviction. Believe in what you are doing. Believe that it is the right thing to do and that it is an action that will ultimately make a difference. It's like I said before, I believe murder to be barbaric, but as a means to protect and preserve the lives of my children and my own, I probably would do whatever it takes. It is the first law of nature, self-preservation, a last-means effort I would hate to have to employ, but a necessary evil as the war-mongers would say, that might be the only means of self-preservation.

Your Word

It all comes down to this: honor your word. I'm fond of the saying that "A man is only as good as his word." It is a tenant I live by and respect and appreciate men who do the same. When we honor our word, we are able to walk in pride and dignity, as men of distinct character. We can sleep good at night, face the world in the morning and never have to attempt to excuse our mistakes to the fault of someone else. You don't have to be perfect or pretend to be. When we honor our word, others are inclined to be more accepting of our imperfections and shortcomings. It doesn't take much to honor your word. Just be deliberate with your action and you'll give honor to your word every time.

INTEGRITY

According to Webster's New College Dictionary 3rd edition, integrity is a firm adherence to a code or standard of values or soundness. Your integrity will, like so many elements of character, be determined by your morals and values. All the sound lessons you learn as you grow that are positive and help set the confine, which governs and directs our behavior. It is a moral standard that is self-imposed.

The most common indicator of an individual's integrity is whether they honor their word. Our word is our bond. It is a pact of sorts that we make with each other every time we communicate. It happens on an even greater scale when we complete unspoken agreements, as in the form of executing civic duties. For example, when a person goes to the doctor or is admitted to an emergency room with an issue, they expect that the individual serving them is going to take care of them. They essentially entrust that person with their life. Not because they know them well or they care about them, but because in our society the duties of a doctor are viewed with great esteem. We trust and believe that the individual will take care of us. It is a duty the doctor accepts as part of their responsibility and acts accordingly. Integrity is the element that allows doctors, civil servants, community leaders and people in general to behave in an appropriate manner in regard to human interaction.

Integrity is another of those silent characteristics that is an internal function externalized by your actions. Like that of a doctor, teacher, or civil servant, an individual's actions will say clearly whether he has integrity or not. Positions of service like a waitress have an automatic level of ethics and a moral standard that comes with the territory. Most have some type of oath that the person swears to that is governed by an element of integrity. By acting in those capacities, we explicitly agree to uphold the integrity and duties of that post. It's all about what you say when you make the promise to carry out the duties of the job you commit to. Not to say that people in covenanted positions may not lack integrity, but to highlight the fact that upholding the integrity of your duties should be a priority when you commit to them.

Your integrity is what will help you do the right thing when no one is looking. It is also what charts the course when there is a question about which direction to take. Perhaps you work at an electronics store as a sales clerk. A few customers enter that are obviously not from this country. The store is a discount bargain store that specializes in selling refurbished goods at a steep discount. None of the merchandise is priced because the usual cliental all know that items usually sell for half retail price. The customers spot a few items that they would like to purchase and bring them to you talking amongst themselves in their best English about the price of the items they are interested in buying. By the time they reach you, the one in the group with the best English asks how much the items are. You could tell them full retail price and pocket the amount over the actual price. You could tell them ten percent off to make them feel they got a deal and still pocket the rest or you could sell it at the half off discounted rate and treat them fairly like everyone else.

Integrity is the element that will help you make the right choice. It is the ethic which you live by that says there is a moral standard that you will not go below or compromise. When we behave with integrity, it makes it hard for others to question your character. Building integrity is a slow and tedious process. At times, it takes situations and circumstances in which your integrity is compromised for you to learn and judge what it means to have integrity. One thing you can be certain of is that if you are willing to cheat and do dishonest things, integrity is definitely an area in which you are lacking.

Integrity is a combination of all the good and positive qualities and characteristics that we will discuss in these pages. It is the final result that others will see in our actions and at times may not even know since much to do with integrity is silent, internal, and personal. So, what's the big deal with displaying integrity if no one is going to directly be able to see and tell that you are rich in integrity?

For starters, it will help solidify your own self-esteem. It is a self-validating mechanism that helps you know that you are of value to society. As well as an unspoken declaration of the same to others that is delivered over time as people make determinations about you based on character assessments.

As always, people are listening to what you say, but more than that, they are watching what you do to make their final judgment about who and what they believe you to be. To behave with integrity says that you have some level of moral standards and ethics that you believe to be important. Sure, the ideals we each hold dear may vary slightly depending on a number of factors. Yet, we should be able to agree that things and element that are positive, productive, healthy, and helpful are universal.

CONTROL

Control is such a seemingly simple concept that is often hard for men to achieve. In fact, control is an element that men are expected to exhibit in their behavior for the most part as much as you can. Something about being male confers the responsibility for controlling not only our behavior, but just about every other element in our surroundings. Control your emotions, attitude, behavior, doings, mouth, circumstances—anything that is in your sphere of influence is subject to your control. It is the passage in the Bible that says, "God gave man dominion over the earth." This is a sign that man is in, or at least, should be in control of things.

The irony of it is that something seemingly so easy to do is more of a challenge than it appears. Real control is the ability to determine when the element of control is out of our hands. The man who is truly in control is the one who knows when to relinquish it in order to remain in control. There will never be a time in life that any one person will be one hundred percent in control of every single thing. Therefore, for any man to stay in complete control, he will have to release it when he is not best suited to handle the situation. The man who cannot relinquish control in critical times of need to another, better suited than he to lead, is truly out of control.

Many men will struggle for power and control of things and situations that they are ill prepared to handle, many times to our, and those close to us, peril and detriment. Think about it like this; no one would board a plan and go up to the cockpit mid-flight and tell the pilot move over "I'm taking over." Besides the fact that post-911 an act like that might get you killed, and definitely prosecuted, it's just not a bright idea. We trust that the individual flying the plane is qualified to perform the task. In that moment, we hand over control of our safety and safe passage to the individual most qualified to handle the task. Likewise, when a child or spouse is critically injured, we don't rush them into the Emergency Room of the hospital and ask for the instruments to perform emergency surgery. No, we rush them to the hospital ER and hand them over to an emergency room surgeon.

Those are easy examples showing how we relinquish control over our lives on a regular and repeated basis. Yet, there are other not-so-obvious times when we should do just the same, times when it might not seem as critical, but which are nonetheless still as important as either of the aforementioned examples. I can remember as a young man my father telling me that, as he said it, "I got mines, you gotta get yours." It didn't make much sense to my undeveloped teenaged mind, but years later, it is clear what he meant by those simple words. He would say it in the context of a perpetual conversation about education he would have with me. I would complain about something I didn't like about the education system and structure. He would counter that he, my teachers, and the whole of the education institution had theirs already. This was his way of reminding me that it was me who needed to cross the threshold at that point.

In a rush and fit to be in control of my own life, I could not differentiate between sacrifice and investment, surrender and compromise. I thought that conforming to regulations was surely compromising and surrendering my ability to be in control of my own life. The reality was that making the sacrifice to conform to the requirements it took to get ahead and advance was an investment. A hard-headed character disposition that would not serve me well at all. It was that same pig-headed foolishness that would be a power struggle for control that I would suffer with for many years thereafter. I believed then and for many years to follow that I was in control of my life and I was at liberty to destroy it if I so felt the need. The sad part about it was that I was then, and still am now, in control. It was the realization that I am responsible for every action and result in my life that brought it into sharper focus.

The major difference between today and back then is that I've learned from many years of being out of control just what real control is. To be in control is to have such a handle on a situation or things in your life as to exert a positive, healthy and productive influence on them. I was the self-imposed victim of Authority Defiance Disorder. Never clinically diagnosed, but given the track record and the characteristics of the disorder, it's safe to say that I had it bad. Consequently, it was by finding myself at the bottom of situation after situation that I came into the knowledge of what control is and how to attain it favorably so that I could advance as opposed to experience setbacks.

The reality check hit me like a knock-out blow from a UFC heavyweight champion one day while incarcerated. The one good thing about prison is that it gives you a lot of time to think. I had broken a rule and found myself in administrative detention (solitary confinement). When you are taken to the hole for an infraction, the officials don't allow you to go back to your living quarters to pack up your personal property. They do it for you. At some point, they bring it to you in the hole so you can get certain select items out of it that you are allowed to have in administrative segregation. It serves a two-fold purpose; one, so you can inventory your things and complain if all your property is not there as well as get things like your address book, books, photos, writing materials, hygiene items and some food items. After all, if you're going to spend an extended stay there, it helps to have books, something to write with and the picture of somebody you love close to you.

As the guard was inventorying my property and passing me items through the tray trap, a small 11/2 x 21/2 slot in the door, I was feverishly picking up the things he threw in while at the same time trying to take stock of what I couldn't get to ensure it was all there. Somewhere in the process I became exhausted of trying to do two things at once and I just gave up looking out the trap. I listened from behind the steel door as he called off items and yelled back "yeah, pass that" as he came to items I wanted and could have. I remember thinking to myself "I'm tired of picking up the pieces of my life." I watched as all the articles I owned at that point fell into a small pile of nothing on the floor in front of me. Worthless junk, in reality, but the only things of material meaning or value to me and my limited confined world at that moment.

Once the tray trap slammed close with a deafening thud, I bent over to collect the pieces of my life, one by one, for the hundredth time. It was there that the reality of how out of control my life was truly became clear. Each time that I had to pick up the pieces of my shattered life was essentially the result of not being able to or knowing when to relinquish control. Those experiences all led me to that day, that situation—a dead end where I had absolutely no control. It was there in that dungeon-like place that I began to understand what control really was, the secret of how to employ it to maximum effectiveness and that the real secret to control is, and always has been, completely in the mind.

The first thing I had to come to terms with was the fact that I was not and would not be in complete control for a good while to come. Then I had to resolve to be content with limited influence over the current conditions I faced. After I got past those two things, I was challenged next with how I could make the most and best use of everything I had at my disposal. In that moment, I was extremely limited, but the infraction that caused me to be there was not so great that I wouldn't get out. So, after that experience was over, I was once again able to have greater latitude in terms of what I could do. I spent that time reading a lot of self-help literature about being proactive. I committed to apply what I learned to the rest of my stay in prison. I would then carry those same habits into my activities in the world when the time came.

I got out of the hole and was sent to an entirely different location to complete my sentence. This was a place that provided me plenty of opportunities to exercise the skill of control. I am only in control of my own actions. However, if and when we can influence the actions and behavior of others, we can control them and the situation as well. For example, if two men are talking and the conversation escalates into a heated argument, if one man strikes the other, who is in control of the situation? The man who is struck by the other is the one in control. Why? Because in his conversation, he was able to provoke the other to hit him. Sure, the individual who actually did the hitting appears to be physically in control of the situation, but physical control is insignificant if you lack mental control; therefore, the true element of control is solely mental. No matter how much it looks like the element of control favors physical dominance, it is only a situation of temporary control at best.

After much trial and error, which has been more error than trial, I have come to understand real control. If and when I am not in a power position, the best practice is to look for an advantage by trying to influence the one who is. In any situation, what you want is your end result. If you can encourage or influence the decision maker to act in a manner that will produce your desired outcome, then you have been effective at controlling the situation. On the other hand, when the time presents itself for you to stand down and allow someone better qualified to be in control, do so. Just like it would be foolish to tell the pilot to let you fly the plane if you don't know how to fly, it is just as unwise to try to be in control of everything all the time. It is equally as foolish to provoke a man with a gun to shoot you to let him know you're not scared. If there is a gun to your head and the threat of death is imminent, it's okay to surrender control.

For many of us, the control lesson is not easily learned. I know I'm a prime example of one who's been taught the lesson very early on only to have to come into the fullness of understanding after many a hard-learned personal setbacks. Even though experience is the best teacher, it is not always necessary to experience something firsthand to learn. It would have been just as good to heed the message years ago about control when my father spoke.

Only, immaturity and ignorance are closely related. As a youth, in my immaturity I had a healthy dose of ignorance to go with it. I have been blessed that not one of the boys to come behind me has been as foolish. Fortunately, they have learned early on the meaning of control, how to apply it, and how to capitalize on it to advance twice as far, twice as fast.

43

SELF-RESPECT

To have self-respect is to hold one's self in high regard. Simply stated, self-respect is a demonstration of an individuals' ability to care for themselves. By respecting yourself, you will limit the instances where you find yourself in an unhealthy, self-degrading, demoralizing or destructive condition. Not to say that self-respect will automatically eliminate those conditions from befalling us, but that it will limit them. The learning curve dictates that we will undoubtedly experience unpleasant growing pains that will entail many of those unhealthy elements that we would all rather do without. They are the lessons that shape and mold our character. However, self-respect is a trait that can help us up and over those negative experiences and conditions that we encounter.

People are made up of three major components, mind, body and spirit/soul. Although self-respect encompasses the total individual, it's important to explore each individually and identify what self-respect means to each.

Mind
When a man respects his own mind, he will guard his thoughts as if they are a place of great treasures and the origin of his every good thing. In so many ways it is. Hence the saying "a thought is the cause of it all." To be as productive and progressive as possible, we must feed ourselves good mental food. It is impossible to claim to respect our thoughts or minds if we do not feed ourselves a steady regimen of positive and healthy thoughts. An important skill to master in our thinking process is the art of taking troubling or challenging experiences and extracting the positive elements to grow out of them. It is that kind of respect for your mind/thoughts that can help make the learning process a lot less challenging and a whole lot more endurable.

Body
The physical aspect of self-respect starts with obvious direct things that have an immediate effect on an individual. How we eat, whether we exercise, how much rest we get. These areas are critical in keeping ourselves physically healthy and balanced. Amazingly though, there are many other self-degrading physical activities that we engage in that we don't even consider being disrespectful to our physical self. Smoking, for example, is an activity that is socially acceptable, extensively promoted and just about one of the greatest disrespects we can do to our body. Smoking is by no means the only self-destructive activity that is heavily promoted and socially accepted. So are alcohol, drug use, unprotected sex, fast

and processed foods in excess, prescription medicines for everything from weight loss to hair growth, and the list goes on and on. . .

The sad reality is that we are not living in a holistic era. We have been conditioned to like our food fast, tasty, in large amounts and made with extremely unhealthy ingredients. If we have a physical defect, a pill, cream, or product can fix it. Blemish on the face, Proactive® can help. Carrying too many extra pounds, Sensa® can help. Hair line receding, Rogaine® to the rescue, and for the guy with enough money, we can put it all back with hair plugs. Can't get it up... Viagra, Cialis, or Lavitra. Whatever your unpleasant flaw, there's a product to cure it. There may be times when there is a legitimate need for a product to help take care of some chronic condition that can be dealt with by no other means. However, when we get too consumed with using a product for every little thing, we get into unhealthy practices that are not good for our physical selves.

In order to truly show respect to our body we must attempt to employ healthy, balanced and holistic physical practices. One part of that consists of resisting the barrage of mental enticements that advertises, promotes, and conditions us to be open to all the things that appear pleasant and convenient. Fast food tastes good and is completely accessible and convenient. The establishments (fast food industry) make sure they are located in high traffic locations and in large enough numbers that you don't have to travel far to reach one. They spend millions of dollars on advertisements so that their product is never too far from your mind and taste buds.

They are not alone. Companies spend big on marketing campaigns to entice us at every turn to try, buy, and frequent their products. Erectile Dysfunction (ED) drugs show pictures of seemingly satisfied couples enjoying life and each other. They subliminally hint that their product can produce the same for you. Weight loss products flaunt size zero to two models, implying that their product is the reason, and what you see is the result. Sports cars, sports drinks, athletic gear, you name it, the product is unimportant—the message is consistent. Our product is what you need to live a rich and full life. Product promotion is by no means the only reason we have such a difficult time finding a place of healthy balance in our mental and physical well-being. It is just one element among many that contributes to the challenges we face.

In order to find a place of balance where mental and physical self-respect can germinate and grow there has to be a systematic deprogramming. A reconditioning of the mind not to be persuaded by all that sparkles and shines. The best practical method to any real and lasting results is taking a holistic approach. The best way to weight loss is eating a healthy diet of whole foods, limiting fast and processed foods, engaging small but consistent physical exercise/activity, and make sure to give the body proper rest. It is a simple prescription that will work for weight loss and/or maintenance. It also works in some cases for issues like blemished skin, E.D., diabetes, high-blood pressure and high cholesterol. Whole living is not a cure all that will somehow just eliminate all your issues at once. It is, however, a measure that can help reduce a number of avoidable issues.

There will be times when no amount of whole, balanced, and healthy living will fix an issue. Then it is appropriate, even advisable, to seek out something to assist with the ailment. If you have been living a balanced lifestyle but have a perpetual acne problem, then it may be time to look to Proactive to relieve the discomfort. A person with Type II diabetes may have to resort to using insulin for getting his blood sugar under control. Those things amount to taking care of and respecting yourself. The suggestion is that you try everything possible to prevent getting to the point of dependence on a product. Then, when all else fails, you do what you must. It is a discouraging sight to see a man who is overweight and borderline diabetic whose doctor has advised him that if he would just lose some weight, he could get his condition under control, ignore that counsel. The unfortunate fact is that it happens all too often.

Self-respect is one weapon in our arsenal that helps us combat the conditions that lead to self-destructive results. We must first identify the numerous elements that act as our enemy in the capacity of respecting our mind and body. As we become aware of what they are, we are better equipped to take corrective measures that will start us on the road to having healthy habits. Combating the messages that are filtered into our psyche daily is an everyday struggle. It is not the comfortable, pleasant, or convenient course of action to take. Even so, doing this is well worth the determination it will take to make the change. The only way to command respect for us from others is to exhibit it for ourselves to others.

Spiritual/Emotional
No conversation about self-respect would be complete without addressing the third element in the trifecta of the human composition. Respect for your emotional and spiritual health largely consists of being cautious and protective of your emotions. To be emotionally sound will require that when you are able to choose, you do not submit yourself to emotionally unhealthy situations or conditions. As a learning experience, it is all right to brave some situations and conditions that are very emotionally distressful. However, anything beyond that is self-imposed torment that will do you no good. Besides, as with other areas of

respect, the only way others will learn to respect you in that capacity is by how they see you treat yourself.

Men are usually not prone or given to showing emotional vulnerability. Yet it doesn't mean that we lack an emotional element. We are human-beings, subject to the human frailty of emotional unrest. The fact that we may not want to recognize or deal with that element does not exempt us from being responsible for caring for that part of our total makeup. That being the case, we must be conscious of our own emotions. It is a prudent practice to take stock of what part our emotions play in who we are, how we act, and how those actions will affect our interpersonal relationships. We may all like to think of emotions as a woman's thing, but the reality is that emotions play a critical part in all our interactions.

Respecting your own emotions means allowing yourself your own feelings so that you are able to go through them. The ability to go through the emotions of a situation will allow you to experience the emotional highs and lows of the situation so that you are able to clearly think about what you are facing. It minimizes the chances that you will act out emotionally or irrationally. You will have your own feelings about everything that happens. The thing that will set you apart from the average man is your ability to be emotionally stable and make decisions based on rationality and objectivity. The only way to find that place of balance is to acknowledge the part of you that is so imperfectly human. To answer your feelings with proper space for them to bounce around until they are not your governing or driving force. With this kind of respect for your emotions you are able to channel them into productive energy that is helpful.

Consequently, self-respecting emotions will reflect and beget the same kind of response. It is the signature behavior that says to others that they will not be able to just treat you any kind of way. When you manage to control your emotions in a dignified and self-respecting manner, it is a clear message to others that you are balanced and demand that others show some level of balance, respect, and consideration for you in that capacity.

As we combine the physical, mental, and emotional elements of self-respect with all the other positive character traits, we create what is needed to have and display self-respecting qualities. It extends to every area of our lives in that by respecting ourselves we are better equipped and able to respect others. If we have been taught the value of carrying ourselves in an honorable, dignified and self-controlled manner, it becomes easy for us to exhibit the kind of character that is admirable. It will ensure that our presence, contribution, and purpose is one of value and need. You, yourself, want to be respected. People seldom show respect to people who will not respect themselves. It is unreasonable to want others to respect you when you won't respect yourself. Self-respect is an intrinsic quality that is manifested in a very external manner.

If there's any question as to what signifies self-disrespecting behavior, consider the following: lack of respect for elders and authority figures. It is a longstanding custom in our culture to respect our elders. There may be times and situations when the actions of elders or authority figures are questionable. Still, based on how our culture values and defines the nature of those relationships, it is better to show respect as long as the situation does not go against your moral belief and standard. Also, consider using profane and vulgar language in everyday conversation as if you have a limited vocabulary. It is unpleasant and offensive to have to be subject to a conversation that consists of more four-letter words than nouns and verbs. Along those same lines, it is even more offensive to hear men talk about women in a negative, degrading, and misogynistic way. People are constantly assessing, sizing up, and making judgments based on how they see us act. By showing a lack of respect for others, you are inadvertently saying that you lack respect for yourself.

Those are just a few things among many that will speak volumes about your level of respect for yourself. Other things like your personal grooming habits are just as important. Wearing your pants slacking off your behind, being in public with any part of your undergarments on display and wearing your hair disheveled are other indicators. You are having a silent conversation with people simply by the way you look out in public. An attitude of indifference in your actions and interactions is another tell-tale sign of your level of self-respect, or lack thereof. Your consideration level, your cleanliness in public domain, even your work ethic will all tell a story of how much respect you have for yourself. Moreover, it will show how you see and value yourself.

For a black boy or man, the single most telling indication of his self-respect level is arguably his use of the "N word!" It has become so socially acceptable that it is no longer just a black male illness. It has gotten to the point that any male minority can freely spew the slur as if it were the equivalent of calling someone by their name. Blacks, Latinos, Indians, Middle Easterners—you name it—except Whites, other than for a rare breed of hip-hop indoctrinates, it is nothing to hear little boys and grown men alike dropping the N-bomb like a squad of fighter jets on an air raid at the start of a war. There is no justification for the behavior. There have been many high-profile people trying to justify the use. Jay-Z tried on Oprah. Tupac tried to legitimize it by creating an acronym for "Never Ignorant

Getting Goals Accomplished." Any number of guys who use the term will try to dismiss their ill-mannered behavior with a number of unacceptable excuses.

The history of the word is itself the clearest and most profound reason why the use of any variation of the word is disrespectful, degrading, and self-destructive. To use something so toxic to identify yourself is not only demoralizing but also self-degrading and a bit idiotic. There is no measure of self-respect in labeling yourself something that historically was used to demean, belittle, and disrespect a person. The original word nigger meant a stupid person. It carries such great historic significance because for so many years it was used as a racial slur to identify black people in belittling and disrespectful terms that it has been removed from many new dictionaries.

There is no way that anyone can believe that mainstream society would consider something so vile that they would attempt to remove its presence from existence yet keep it alive by using it as a nickname and think it's self-respecting. There is no dignity in branding yourself a fool. There is no pride, no integrity, no honor— there is no distinction in running afoul of yourself. In order to preserve a modicum of self-respect, no black male, boy or man, can refer to himself as "nigga" and be content. Set a standard for yourself. Don't refer to yourself as such and demand that others don't either.

In the book *The New Jim Crow*, Attorney Michelle Alexander attempts to explain why black men would embrace the stereotype of the "gangsta culture" if it could cause issues for them like racial profiling. In her explanation, she makes some good points that I believe lends some clarity to the possible reason so many black males use the N-word. She writes the following:

> "There is absolutely nothing abnormal or surprising about a severely stigmatized group embracing their stigma. Psychologists have long observed that when people feel hopelessly stigmatized, a powerful coping strategy—often the only apparent route to self-esteem—is embracing one's stigmatized identity. Hence, "black is beautiful" and "gay pride"— slogans and anthems of political movements aimed at ending not only legal discrimination, but the stigma that justified it. Indeed, the act of embracing one's stigma is never merely a psychological maneuver; it is a political act—an act of resistance and defiance in a society that seeks to demean a group based on an inalterable trait. As one gay activist once put it, "Only by fully embracing the stigma itself can one neutralize the sting and make it laughable."

Could that also be the case with the N-word? A type of desensitizing through acceptance. I can see the value and validity in black people embracing the word in order to take the power and sting out of it so that it could no longer be used as a weapon against them. In fact, over the ages we have somehow found a way to twist the social significance amongst ourselves in order to give the word an element of exclusivity. It has given us a one up on White America that has been derived from centuries of their offensive and oppressive behavior that they now have no control over. It's an understandable mentality but flawed at best. The oppression of the slave masters is over. The only remnants that still exist are those that we continue to extol in our attempts to resist and defy a society that is more accepting now more than ever.

Self-respecting behavior requires a level of selfishness. It means you will need to be conscious of yourself. You must insulate yourself from destructive forces and elements. As with referring to yourself in derogatory terms, you must first love you enough that you do not want to identify yourself in an unflattering way. You must be selfish enough to remove yourself from people, places and things that are not consistent or in agreement with the things you believe and value. You must be selfish enough that you will feed yourself good messages about yourself, your purpose, your contribution and your self-worth, ensuring that the input into your physical, mental, and emotional self is healthy and balanced. That type of self-respecting selfishness is the type it takes to make you valuable to the people around you.

By respecting yourself you are able to realize the value of real self-worth. It boosts and maintains your self-esteem. When you believe in yourself, you are more confident in your abilities. That confidence aids you in your ability to make significant and lasting contributions to your family, friends, and community.

RESPECT

Respect is similar to self-respect in that all the same components apply. The difference being, respect is an external exchange that we share with one another. It is a level of consideration that we exhibit to others in our interpersonal interactions. If you have mastered the art of self-respect, respect will be the material outgrowth. Consider the previous examples of self-disrespecting behavior; disrespect of elders and authority figures, vulgar language, misogynistic behavior, and the others. These are all behaviors that are predicated on how an individual carries himself. In discussing the behavioral traits that were indicative of self-respect, we automatically covered the area of giving and showing respect.

It's not necessary to revisit a long, detailed essay on respect. Let me just point out a few things to remember in sight of the next level of the respect mold. Respect, simply stated, is to extend to others the same quality treatment that you maintain for yourself. It requires you to care for others the same as you do yourself. You must be attentive and responsible for the same elements for others as you are for yourself. Yes, there are different levels of respect. Some are more intimate than others, but in general we should extend a standard level of respect to all people regardless of who they are.

When we go out to a restaurant to eat with our family, we don't just show up at the place and demand we be seated right away at the next available table. We check in with the hostess, get in line with the other patrons and wait for a table to come available. When we are in the grocery store and we're done shopping, we find a check-out line and wait our turn to be serviced. In the barber shop, airport, school, everywhere we go, we respect the customary "wait your turn" protocol. It is an element of respect we extend not because we care about the people that were there before us, but more so because we've been taught that we should treat others the way we want to be treated. It is a generic respect that is bred by default in the many lessons we are taught as kids, the ones that start at home when we're young, continue through school age and are pretty firmly grounded by our late teens. It's that kind of respect that serves us well in our everyday exchanges in the outside world.

The more intimate respect is reserved mostly for people who hold a place of significance in our lives. Spouses, children, parents, family, friends, and the like; the relationships that have some type of mental/emotional effect on us. In these relationships, the respect factor takes on different dynamics. In relationships, an individual has to be conscious, cautious and considerate of another's mental, physical and emotional health and well-being. Our intimate relationships are the most meaningful. They are the ones that give us the greatest joy and the most pain. By respecting others in our intimate relationships, we create a healthy environment.

A key element that is indicative of respect for our intimate relationships is listening to our loved ones. Listening tells the other person that you are concerned about them. It says that how they feel, what they think, and what they want makes a difference to you. It also gives you the input you need to make the right choices concerning the direction you should take in the dealings between you and that person. People are always happy to know that you have given them ample and just consideration in your decision-making process when they have some interest in the decision being made. The first and best way to get the necessary information to make sure that consideration is made is to listen to that individual.

A lot of respect for others is shown by simply being considerate. This is the forethought of how your actions will affect others. Are you speaking in a way that is positive, appreciative, and edifying or is your conversation negative, profane, vulgar and one-sided? Will you give up your seat so an elderly person can sit down? Will you get the door for a person coming with their arms full of packages? These are all small signs that an individual has respect for other people. Respect is a small token behavior that has such a great return on investment. In most cases when a person gives others respect it will be returned. Sure, there will be occasions when we will give respect only to be met with capricious behavior in return. Those are times when you will be called to exercise control not only over yourself but over the offending party as well. In those instances, you must remember your self-respecting tenets and let them be your guide. Anything less would be to allow the offender to have control over you and your behavior.

LOYALTY

Loyalty is a quality that is centered around a man's ability to be true to something or someone. To be loyal to a person is to exhibit some level of commitment, fidelity, and faithfulness to the relationship. Likewise, loyalty to a cause consists of much the same elements. It is the condition of transitioning from the 'I' state of being to the state of commitment to others. To be loyal to someone or something takes deliberate action. We are living in the most connected/disconnected time in history. Never before have we been so accessible and disconnected as we are today. Cell phones, social media, teleconferencing, IM's and email have us linked up in every way except being face-to-face. It has given way to a condition I like to think of as, accessible but disconnected.

Communication experts say that communication is about thirty percent what you say and seventy percent everything else. Tonality, delivery, and body language are the bulk of communication; the luxury of which most modern means of communication don't provide. The side effect of our new condition is that much of our conversation gets lost in translation and is simply left to the interpretation of the recipient. This new condition has birthed a new era of more self-indulged people. As the condition of self-indulgence grows, it becomes harder and harder to be loyal to things outside of ourselves. If we concentrate too much on ourselves and our own desires, the condition of loyalty will become increasingly harder to produce. Of course, the modern marvel of multiple avenues of access is not responsible for whether we learn and maintain loyalty in our relationships. It is simply one of numerous ingredients in a collective of new conditions that make it more challenging today to learn and exercise loyalty in our relationships.

Provided you were taught lessons of selflessness, commitment, consideration, respect and the many other positive qualities indicative of a real man's behavior, you won't find loyalty to be so hard to produce. However, given the interpersonal disconnect, you may have to be more deliberate and attentive to that element as you engage your interpersonal relationships. That might not always be the easiest thing to do either, especially since the people closest to you may not have your same value system and may not reciprocate loyalty in kind. If this happens, it is best to reevaluate the relationship to determine the value of keeping that person close to you.

Granted, you will not have the luxury of choosing some relationships. You don't get to choose your parents, siblings or other family members, but beyond that, most others are by choice. Then there are the outside relationships that are beyond your control such as school, work, and general public interactions. However, the latter do not entail a deeply intimate level or element of loyalty, whereas the former do. To be loyal to something is a strong statement of allegiance. It says that you are so committed to that person or cause that you are willing to be hurt on behalf of it. When you give something that kind of dedication and attention. you want to make sure it is worthy of what you are committing. All things may not be worth the allegiance you pledge when you give your loyalty to something.

This is a rule that applies across the board. You must examine every relationship, from the casual to the most intimate and determine which are deserving of your loyalty, and which are not. There may be instances when a family member may not be worthy of your loyalty and a co-worker is. Just know that if you give or have given your loyalty to someone or something, you are giving it a very dear and valuable piece of your heart. If that thing is not worth your loyalty and you come to find out after the fact you will suffer great pain as a result. The best practice when it comes to loyalty is to carefully examine every situation, person, and thing thoroughly before you make such a grave commitment. Be selective with whom and what you commit to. Lastly, do not overextend your loyalty to too many things. To do so is to invite a potential emotional crisis later down the line.

I can think of a few things and people I extended my loyalty that, in hindsight, honestly didn't deserve it. It's part of the reason I can speak with such clarity and resolve about how one should evaluate and exact loyalty. Honestly, someone can be told all the best and right things about loyalty and still miss the point. Unfortunately, loyalty is one of those characteristics best learned by firsthand experience. Just be forewarned that the lesson of lost loyalty is a lesson that is served cold. It will not take many instances wherein one extends a hand of loyalty that is met with anything other than loyalty back before it is discovered. I'd be so bold as to say that it will not take many more than two occasions of another misappropriating the loyalty in a relationship before you will become ultra-selective about who you extend your loyalty to.

The great thing about the loyalty factor is that once you've determined who those people or causes are, you will likely cement your commitment, giving those very few select things a priority order and level; usually pretty high. It's helpful to remember the accessible but disconnected example and know that you are fighting against elements of separation that are powerful and absolutely unhelpful trying to foster loyalty in relationships. Even so, loyalty is an important quality that you cannot afford to compromise or go without. Even when it looks like an antiquated practice in an era that seems to be getting more self-indulgent by the minute, your ability to go beyond the 'me' to the 'we' frame of thinking is critical. It could be the element that spells out greatness in you. Can you imagine what today would look like if Dr. King was not loyal to the cause of civil rights in America?

TRUST

Trust is a fragile commodity. It is in so many instances taken for granted. For the most part, trust is almost a given in our interpersonal relationships. People tend to give others the benefit of the doubt in believing that what you see is what you get in terms of trust. Unless someone does something that causes a person to distrust them, we will generally extend a person a basic amount of trust in the beginning of our dealings in a general sense. We are, however, living in a time in which it is getting harder to just extend trust on face value. To that I say, all meaningful levels of trust will need to be earned over time. After there has been enough experience, then cement the value of trust between yourself and the people you choose to be involved with.

Keeping with the first confines of trust beginning and being in your family ties, it is worth examining how it develops and plays out in that structure. Having a healthy concept of trust in your family environment will set a good foundation for the rest of your personal dealings. The best relationship to look at that in most cases epitomizes trust is the parent-child relationship. Kids trust their parents unequivocally. This is a condition that does not soon change unless the parent gives the child numerous reasons not to trust over an extended period of time. It is in that same vein that as adults we will extend that same kind of preliminary trust to others, provided they don't exhibit some kind of character defect or behavior that causes us to question their trustworthiness.

Trust is a fragile element. It can be lost faster than it can be gained and is hard to rebuild if it is ever abused or lost. It is easy to abuse someone's trust. I can still remember how it felt to find out that my mother withheld information from me that I asked about as a young boy. At the time, she didn't believe I was old enough or mature enough to understand, and when I asked, she gave me what she deemed was an age appropriate answer. The challenge was that when I did finally come of age to know the full extent of the situation I was questioning, I felt deceived by the half-truth I had been told. Back then, I considered what I was told as being the equivalent of a lie. I developed trust issues like being unable to trust law enforcement officials or having my dad to turn to for protection from injustice. Each little abuse or betrayal of trust built a tougher shell of callous that became hard to penetrate the older I got.

When a person loses the ability to trust on a fundamental level, it makes establishing all other relationships much harder. We become skeptical of people, their intentions and motives. It is always prudent to examine those things about a person anyway, but a fundamental lack of trust will many times not even allow you to get that far. It takes a lot of energy to maintain a guarded disposition in your openness to trust. We do not live in a world where you can survive without being dependent on someone. This means at some point we will have to trust somebody. To lack trust on such a fundamental level as I did is to set yourself up for a great deal of heartache and headache.

Trust is what gives us the ability to believe. If we trust something is true, we will believe it. That's why on a fundamental level we need to make sure we are careful to guard the trust factor in all our relationships like it is a valuable asset. The truth is that it is an invaluable asset that, once broken or violated, may be next to impossible to get back. I believe trust to be so important in our interpersonal dealings that very early on I made an internal resolve to always be straight up with people, even at times at the expense of taking the chance that the recipient would take offense. The rationale was if I were always honest, I would not give people any reason not to trust my word. In the process, I made a lot of bad decisions in sometimes telling more than I should, but one thing was for damn sure, if I said it, it was sure to be the truth. In fact, somewhere around fifteen years old, I had completely internalized the need to either tell the truth or hold your tongue. That's not to say that I didn't do questionable things that could or would jeopardize my intimate and personal relationships. It just means that I would plead the fifth if I was questioned about it.

To be honest, the truth lessons came at the expense of messing up a lot of meaningful intimate relationships. A great many of them were romantic, but just as many were between family and friends as well. When we allow our intimate relationships to be jeopardized or compromised, we end up paying an awfully high price. Not only are they hard to repair, but the process is a hurtful experience. The feeling that one gets when one's trust has been betrayed is just as unpleasant as physical torture. Torture is a constant repetitive action designed to torment the recipient. Betrayal of trust has the same effect—only mental. It is a constant display in your mind that this person does not have your best interest at heart. The worst part being that most of the time for someone to misappropriate the trust of another, there is likely some level of intimate connection between the two. This also means that they will likely have deep feelings about the situation.

Overall, trust is an element that it's better not to lose in the first place. Considering the fragility and value of trust, the best thing for us to do in our relationships is to look for every way to protect, strengthen, and reaffirm the trust factor in all we do. In the event a situation has gotten out of hand and needs damage control, look for the best action that will help reestablish what has been

57

compromised. The earning and keeping of trust should rank high on a man's priority list.

STRENGTH

The concept of strength amongst men is grossly misrepresented. As a matter of fact, it can take on numerous different dynamics depending on who is making the determination. So many things factor into what we believe the definition of strength to be. Strength is the ability to withstand the challenges of life without succumbing to the pressures. I love the idea that men are supposed to be strong, like in unit measurements of how much weight you can lift. However, I fear that we may have a faulty concept of what distinguishes and measures real strength in a man.

Physical vs. Mental
The first show of strength, and easiest to see of course, is physical. If a man can bench press 315 lbs., squat 405, or dead lift 650, it is obvious that he is physically strong. Nobody would question or second guess it. His strength is on display for anybody in his immediate vicinity to see. Better yet, we don't need to see him work out to be able to determine his strength. His body would probably say just as loudly as a lifting demonstration. His frame would prove by his muscular build that he is a strong guy. This is a condition that our culture grants a great deal of significance—how physically strong you are.

Physical strength is synonymous with dominance, which happens to be an inborn condition of dominance with which men are hard-wired. It almost seems natural that we crave physical strength to complement our natural urge to dominate the things in our physical space. Because physical strength and dominance are parallel traits, they basically work in tandem making men one step above an ape insofar as the strength thing goes, hence the saying, "going ape-shit," yet with a bit more ability to rationalize and reason, of course.

One would think that the ability to reason would help govern and guide us in a positive direction in the strength department. That is not always the case. The proof is in the many instances when we men do stupid things just to prove that we can take on a challenge, and, consequently, that we are strong because of it.

Culturally, it is a truly American trait to put our strength on display. It happens on all levels; in our politics and the way our elected officials treat others in world affairs. Our foreign relations diplomacy goes something like, "do not test us or there will be a price to pay." This is confirmed and reaffirmed by statements like, "we don't negotiate with terrorists," or "we will hunt you down, find you, and serve justice." There is no question or doubt about how we present ourselves in world affairs and foreign relations. The disposition doesn't much change for any other aspect of America the Great, America the Strong. The Olympic games, education, business, the wealth of the nation all have very well-defined characteristics of a culture shrouded in a strength mentality.

That conditioning in the macro environment makes it easy for us to get a seriously skewed perspective on the real meaning of strength. Even in our microenvironments, we are confronted by an ideology of strength that is a misrepresentation. We have all experienced the social pressure in our community, peer group and other sources that have made predefined determinations of manly behavior. People characterize certain behavior as weak and other behavior as strong. It can lead us to believe untruths like a man is not strong if he cowers away from a physical confrontation or he is weak if he shows too much emotion in any given situation. Not just any kind of emotions, but sensitive emotions. Rage, anger, aggression—these are types of emotions, but not the kind that will get a man labeled as weak. In fact, the latter are all behaviors that can add to the illusion of superficial strength.

All said, men put entirely too much emphasis on our external shows of strength. This is probably because we fear being perceived as weak by others, thereby causing us to cast an external image that we believe others will perceive as strong. There is nothing wrong with being physically strong. Nor is there anything wrong with carrying yourself in a way that exhibits that fact definitively. The challenge is not getting so caught up in the physical nature of strength and keeping in mind that the most important element of strength is internal. It is one that you cannot see but is the governing driver of a man who is in control himself. The man who has mastered his mental strength has conquered one of man's greatest challenges.

Mental fortitude is the characteristic of being truly strong in all respects. Mental strength can aid you in times and situations when physical strength is of no help at all. Your mental strength will establish and determine your will. Your will is an element that can, and many times will, be your driving force. There is no way to see or know a man's mental strength by looking at him. It is an element that can only be seen by observing his actions over an extended period. One must challenge his thoughts to see how mentally strong a man is. There are some small elements that will hint at a man's mental strength, but to make a thorough assessment, it is important to observe him for a longer time.

Does he have the ability to make a resolution and stick to it? Does he have a vice or vices that he tries to stop but always end up succumbing to it over again? Does he keep his word to himself and others? These are all little things that we

60

can observe about a man and tell a good bit about his mental strength. Yet, the best determinant of a man's mental strength is his ability to stay true to his morals, values, and beliefs. A lot of times our surrounding environment is in direct conflict with our standards. If we are able to remain grounded and firm in our own standards, then we, in turn, exhibit a level of mental strength that is self-evident. That's why in all we do, we should be careful to use correct means of judging a man's strength. If we lean to the side of considering the proper measure of determining mental strength over the physical, I'd venture to say that we could create a condition by which we demystify what the real meaning of what strength is. Ask yourself, what would tomorrow look like if all men were taught early on that true strength is mental?

Cultural Variations

Earlier we spoke about the American cultural distinction of strength and on a smaller scale the microelement of community and close surroundings. Something that is personal to me, as well as noteworthy to mention, is the idea of strength that is uniquely African American. More specifically, the urban/hip-hop cultural variation. This one has been popularized by a very negative stereotype. It has demonized its inhabitants by casting a bad boy "thugged-out" image. It is kept alive by passing a derogatory image of the individuals who choose to associate with it, not to mention the prerequisite that you must be hard and strong in order to be considered real.

The strength concept has never been more misinterpreted than by the people who subscribe to the street-life mentality and lifestyle. The common tone in that community about strength is aggressive, dominating and almost always on most fronts physical. This individual does not give too much credence to the tenet of mental strength. In fact, in some cases mental strength in that circle or element can be perceived as weakness. The numerous things the lifestyle promotes is the greatest testament to the fact that mental strength is not highly prized or respected. The lack of respect for authority, rules, hard work, and people are all signature features that indicate a lack of mental strength. Each of these things takes effort and a good bit of mental strength to produce. These are things individuals in that lifestyle and mentality don't seem to take too seriously.

Not all African American males are affected by the influence of the urban/hip-hop culture. There are many boys and men who are far removed from that mentality and condition. However, for the few who are, it's worth saying that there is no future in the front. The show of that kind of behavior is a facade that has been created. It is popularized by entertainment and perpetuated by characters who have no idea what a real man's characteristics are. There is no such thing as being hard. Hard does not denote strength, but ignorance. Hard is a condition of wearing a callous exterior that has nothing to do with strength in and of itself.

To find strength, you will have to dig deep inside to find the part of you that can be silently strong, to face each situation that life hands us in a tempered manner. The separation must be made between physical and mental strength and which of the two is most important.

The lesson of strength is that only the strong survive. Survivors are those who are time tested and have managed to exercise mental strength over their situations and circumstances. Time honored individuals will last the long haul. Physical strength can only carry a man so far. When he is physically exhausted, he has nothing left if he is not able to dig deep into his mind to carry him the distance that his muscles cannot. The real display of strength is not in what a man does or has done, but a lot of the time it is the result of what he doesn't or won't do.

LOVE

The way I see it love is the greatest treasure of life. I have tried to stand on love in every facet of my life. I have used love as my help faction when there was no other element at my disposal. Love has helped me develop a healthy respect for everything around me. I love this earth, so I have agreed to do my part to respect and protect it, to recycle, not be wasteful, live out of necessity and not excessive consumption. These are practices that I attempt to keep at all times because I love and appreciate this earth. I love my family. I try to do all in my power and limited understanding to do what is best for them. I try to stay attentive and observant to their physical, mental and emotional needs. My goal is to make the best choices for them as far as my input and influence is concerned.

The same goes for my friends, and on a larger scale my community and the public at large. It is the element of love that allows me to engage each of these things on grounds that make our interactions high quality. The idea of love in my mind and heart is so grand that trying to explain it in words always seems to be inadequate. However, in the absence of any other means to convey a message (especially in a book), it is all I have. As I've said before, I'm a big believer in judging a person on their actions. Therefore, in evaluating the nature and amount of an individual's love, I believe that a man will speak the amount of his love not in the words he says but in the actions he shows. To say that you love something or someone is meaningless if your actions display something to the contrary.

Love is likely the greatest gift people can give to one another. There are different types but one that covers them all. There is romantic love, like the one that lovers share. There is brotherly love, like the one family and friends share. Then there is what's considered a Godly love. The type of love that entails having love for everything in existence, even things that you might not like so much. Agape or Godly love is the greatest love of them all. It also encompasses the others. Romantic and brotherly love are usually defined by a person having some intimate connection to people they care about. You choose your lover. You choose your friends. Your family is not your choice but a condition that, in most cases, you grow to love over time by virtue of sharing so many intimate experiences. Of course, you can grow to disdain some of those relationships as well, but for the most part, your level of romantic and brotherly love is determined by your contentment in those relationships. Agape love on the other hand is love that is extended beyond your own personal feelings and beneficial interest in the relationships.

The lesson of Agape love is best told through religious means. Although the concept is not necessarily relegated to religious confines. The passage in the scriptures that says "love the Lord your God with all your heart. Then love your brother as you love yourself," is the best way to paraphrase agape love in short order. It is not necessary to be given to any religious dogma to be able to benefit from the power of the command. The value is in the belief that love for something greater than yourself will help ground you. That if you love yourself, and everything just as much as you do yourself that you will bring humanity the greatest gift that you have to offer.

When we have and give that level of love to others it is easy for us to actively exchange all levels of love in our interpersonal relationships. The qualities of love are many. There are some more important than others. The one that I think is most noteworthy is that real love is unconditional. In order to say and mean that you love someone you must not place conditions on your love. It cannot be predicated on the conditions or circumstances that surround you. It does not mean you automatically have to put up with or accept conditions that are intolerable just because you love someone. It only means that you keep loving that individual regardless of the changes the relationship may take.

The Give and Take
Love is not complete without a reciprocating factor. It is the give and take exchange that makes love complete. Anything less is not really love, it is abuse. If one person gives another love without getting it in return, that relationship is parasitic. It is not a situation that is healthy. The individual that is giving love without being loved in return does so at the peril of his own emotional health. There will be relationships that will present a one-sided element of love that is not reciprocated. It is not a cause to stop loving that individual, but rather love them from a healthy distance that will not emotionally drain you.

Determining how and when to give love is not an easy process. Love in and of itself is a tricky situation. Ideally, we would agree on what love consists of and how we should distribute it. Except, we live in a less-than-perfect world and rarely, if ever, are we presented with ideal anything. Therefore, determining the appropriateness of our love exchange will rely on 1) the things we value, 2) how we view and regard love itself and 3) how we see, value, and regard the relationship in question. Largely, this means that the defining factors in the love valuation in our interpersonal relationships will vary tremendously. No two of us will see the defining characteristics of love the same. We will need to find the place in each of our relationships where we feel comfortable with the love exchange as it is reciprocated. Our relational interactions will be the circumstances that will help us to not only learn and appreciate the love element, but also define it as well. Love is our binding agent. It is what holds our interpersonal relationships together. Without it, we would have ceased to exist a long time ago. It is an action that in many ways is just as innate as it is learned. Like the maternal relationship between mother and child—the bond begins as soon as the child is conceived. It is a bond that continues to grow over time as the two grow together. Behavioral scientists have concluded that people who are not shown and given the proper love and affection as children can grow to develop serious emotional challenges later on in life. It is just one small reminder of how and why love is so important in our relationships and lives.

Knowing the power and effect love has on the quality of our lives, it is important that we attempt to establish a clear definition of love. Some of us may not have had the most ideal circumstances in our lives growing up. There may have even been times when the examples and experiences endured were counter-productive in terms of what one would consider healthy examples of love. Those experiences, as unfortunate as they were, are already done. There is no way to reverse or erase them from our past. The best we can do going forward is to reassess any unhealthy past experiences that have had adverse effects on our ability and capacity to love and look for ways to use those experiences to improve our current conditions.

That is not an easy process. It is one that will likely take a lot of interpersonal evaluation. It will definitely take a great level of selflessness and an extreme willingness to forgive. One of my own greatest challenges in finding that place of well-defined measures of love is in what I consider my greatest failure, the abandonment of my own children. It is one of those counter-productive experiences that is, by all means, unhealthy. I have questioned myself over and over after every phone conversation, the close of every visit, and the salutations of every letter where I said I love you—how could that statement be true? In my mind, the things that love consists of do not fit the circumstances I have had to endure as a result of my deeds. Yet, my heart speaks loudly confirming and reaffirming my mind that yes, I do indeed love my children.

The actions that caused my temporary absence were based on my ignorance. I was doing at the time what I believed I needed to do to give my children what they needed physically and materially. At no time did I stop to think about the consequences or the costs or risk. In all my evaluations of my behavior, I firmly believed that I was doing what was necessary to provide for my children.

I am a simple man. I don't need extravagant things. Beyond the basic necessities, the only thing material goods are good for in my opinion is to enhance the quality of interpersonal experiences we share with the people we love. In my past, I did things that today I'm not too proud of. I did them in order to supply the things I thought were necessary to make those experiences the best and most memorable they could be. I dealt drugs to support two minor children at a critical juncture in my own life. I was eighteen, I had just gotten shot in the back and paralyzed. I had one son who was about to turn two, and I soon found out that another was born within months of my incident. My life was different after that. I had two little major responsibilities on my hands. From all that I had been taught until that point, I had to take responsibility and man up. No amount of feeling sorry for myself and my new condition was going to change that. My mother had driven home the point long before that when I was grown enough to make a child, I better be man enough to care for it.

I had just barely gotten a GED and I didn't have one marketable skill to my name. I got on Social Security Supplemental Income (SSI), signed up for all the government subsidized programs available and set out on my own to try to navigate the seas of adulthood. I signed up for Vocational Rehabilitation (VR) training program which paid to send me to community college and gave my best go at getting back into the world being as active and productive as I could. At the time, SSI was paying $465 a month. My other expenses were based on my income, so I could have the bare essentials with the little assistance I was getting.

As school started the next fall, I was fortunate enough to receive a car as a gift from my mother's ex-husband (my stepdad) so I could get back and forth to school. The bills started to accumulate. Car insurance, day care for my oldest son; gas, food, other childcare necessities started to consume the $465 each month just as soon as I would get it. Shortly after, I found out I had another son. The news didn't help my situation. The discovery only meant that what little I did have left was about to be consumed along with all the rest. I tried to focus on the bigger picture, reminding myself that this wouldn't be the condition forever. Eventually, I would be finished school, working and making a sustainable living myself, and this struggle would all be a part of my story about how I overcame the impossible.

Life did not take the same course of the plans I had mapped out. Caring for two babies at once cost more than my income. I felt obligated to make up the missing ends in the middle and resorted to something I knew would make that possible. Milk, diapers, clothes, childcare, rent, gas, and everything else was expensive, so I started selling weed to meet the need. It was a constant balancing act with school, picking up the boys, getting home to do homework, both theirs and mine,

66

feeding them and sitting with them until their mothers picked them up. It was an *everyday* job. Then dipping out late into the night trying to make a dollar out of .15¢ was like putting in overtime. I continued on like that until about two years later my youngest son's mother called saying she needed me to keep our two-and-a-half-year-old son for a while until she got herself together. I went to get him. It was a position I was ill prepared to be in, but one I believed I was obligated to assume.

Now a full-time parent of a two-year-old, and a part-time to a four-year-old, I had to make some life-changing decisions, and fast. I finally resolved to postpone school until the boys were a little older, at least ten more years. By then, they would be fourteen and twelve, old enough to stay at home alone, and I could go to school while they did, work at night and be home at a decent hour to share a little time with them during the week. That settled the dilemma. What it didn't settle is how I would support them in the meantime. Without any employable skills to my credit or the ability to secure them at that moment, I continued to do what seemed like it was necessary to get by.

I didn't see many avenues to make the provisions. I felt like I would do whatever was necessary to make sure I provided for my kids with their needs, and in some cases their desires. I loved them so much that I would have given anything to make sure that they had quality experiences as they were growing up. At the time, it all seemed like the right thing to do. I didn't drive a flashy car; I drove a family car. I didn't wear designer clothes or jewelry; I shopped at discount stores like TJ Maxx and bought things on sale. I didn't frequent clubs or blow money trying to impress friends or attract women. I saved my money and spent it on things like family get togethers, supporting my boys, and making sure their travel experiences where culturally diverse, rich, and truly memorable. In my mind, it was what love was all about. A quality of life that was rich in interpersonal interactions and exchanges, not material things.

In my limited understanding and view, I thought what I was doing was the epitome of love. Then before the ten-year period was over, I hit a dead end. The consequences of my behavior bit me on the butt, and the life that I had provided until that point was abruptly halted. I fell into legal challenges that threatened the future of everything around me, including the two principle reasons I was involved in doing what I was that had caused my issue in the first place. Because I chose to deal drugs to sustain our lives, I was facing a lengthy prison stay. I still rationalized in the beginning that it was what I had to do, and I did it out of love. It didn't take long for that fallacy to fade and I began to question what love truly was. After being gone from my children for so much time, I began to see how horribly wrong my judgment had been all along. What I believed I was doing in love was misguided. It was more destructive than helpful.

 Love has nothing to do with the amount of high-quality experiences or material things you provide. It has all to do with you being present and available to help guide and develop your children into healthy individuals. This is the very thing that I ended up depriving my children of. It is that reality that still causes a disturbance of anguish inside me. I know I love my boys, but the act of abandoning them is always in conflict with my mind, begging the question—how much could I love them if I let something like that happen? They may not struggle with this as much as I do, or maybe they do. I can only say for sure that no burden has ever been greater in my life. It is one thing to mess up my own life. It is something incomprehensible to inflict such unjust damage in the life of a child.

This is one of those experiences I spoke about that is counter productive. One that I can no more erase than I can reset and do over. The lesson I have learned has been invaluable. There is nothing in this world more important than being available for the people you love. I can't answer how my children should internalize their own experiences or how they should react because of it. I can only encourage that they do not allow the experience to stifle them from going forward in their own lives. In certain respects, we both have an element of overcoming to do. I have to relinquish the baggage of the guilt that accompanies what I have done. Each of them must personally deal with how he feels about my absence, where they believe my love stands, and how they will grow from and through this experience.

In so many ways this will be the catalyst and cornerstone of their own sentiments of what love is and what it means to them. Whether they say that my absence was the worst experience they ever felt and don't ever wish to abandon anyone they love, or whether the absence creates a greater value for the ability to have and access a loved one, it will surely be a major development that will have lasting effects on their future definition of love.

In the end, the reality is that love is all we have. When there are no more material things, nice dinners out, event-filled trips out of town or out of the country—love is all that's left. Be it in the stillness of your thoughts about the memories you have from those experiences or the depths of your heart after a loved one has passed on and memories are all you have left, no amount of material anything will replace love. Only love can keep your bond intact for you.

It has been an experience of extreme distance and separation that has helped me understand the true meaning and value of love. It is a sacrifice that was not worth the tradeoff. I would give anything to get back the time I've lost with my children. Since I know that's not possible, I must pick up the pieces of our shattered experience and try to put them back together in a way that signifies as well as solidifies that I really do love them. It is the driving force behind these numerous pages; to say that I love you as well as what is important to me, to ensure you all have a clear idea and knowledge of who your father really is. I have not been able to give you the gift of my presence, so I want to give you the next best thing—the gift of my thoughts.

I learned the best lesson of love from religion. As I have grown, I have put some distance between myself and the limitations of religious doctrine. In its place, I have adopted love as my religion. This is a hard-taught lesson that continues to evolve and mature with each day that I am blessed to be alive. A lesson that I must admit has been best taught in the one relationship that I consider to be the greatest of them all. The parent-child relationship is one where the parent is charged with teaching the child, or the children, the lessons of life. In our experience, I must concede that you all have been the greatest teachers I have ever known.

CARING

The nature of caring is to be concerned about something or someone to some measure. There are varying degrees of caring and numerous different things one can care about, but the most significant of them is our concern with, and caring for, each other. This is followed very closely by our concern with, and about, situations and conditions that affect us directly and indirectly. For the moment, we will direct our focus on the significance of caring in our personal relationships.

Why Should We Care?
In light of the way people have changed and evolved, it is becoming increasingly more important for us to be conscious of one another. Remember the condition accessibly disconnected? Our modern era has developed in such a way that the interpersonal connection that once existed has developed a growing divide, the gap in which continues to grow larger and larger by the minute. In times past, when people didn't have as many media of communication between them, we were much more careful how we engaged each other in communication. It made it a little easier to be conscious and considerate of how other would receive us. If someone had something of a sensitive nature to share with another, they would likely look for the most gentle way to express their thoughts. Communicating in person, or even on the telephone, comes with all kinds of communicating extras that cannot be expressed in media like text, email, social media and so on.

People have to take a number of different variables into consideration when communicating in person. How will they be received? How do they feel about the person? Do they value the relationship? How will the recipient receive the message? Will they react with hostility or violence? These are all critical elements in communicating and nurturing healthy relationships. The fact that we have become accustomed to communicating via numerous media that don't afford us the luxury of those essential and critical elements makes the need for us to be aware, conscious, and deliberate about caring all the more urgent.

Consider the effect our modern means of communicating have had on our interpersonal exchanges and ability to care. Social media, for example, is a platform of communication. Not only do our friends and family have access to us through it, but the rest of the world does too. Why is this so important? I was talking to my mother about something one of my boys had posted on his Facebook page that was, shall we say, vulgar. Her solution was to send him a private message reminding him that his great grandmother and great aunt were his online friends—a nice way to say "check your roguish behavior." Needless to say, I don't think it mattered much because shortly after that she was telling me about some other unflattering posts he'd made.

This is just a small example of why we must be conscious of caring, especially with regards to others. If I had to guess, I'd probably say that my son did not mean to purposely offend or disrespect anyone by his tasteless posts. I imagine if he was standing in front of his great aunt or great grandmother talking to his brother or peers, he would not have dared to say in person what he thoughtlessly scribbled on his Facebook page. This is the difference between person to person and accessibly disconnected communication.

All the elements that are essential in communication like tonality, non-verbal's like body language and facial expressions and other gestures that communicate thoughts are lost in translation in our various communication means. We are then charged with the responsibility of caring and concern in order to be conscious of the small things like not disrespecting our elder family by some ill-spoken comment on social media.

Most of us say we care about our family, friends, community, and any number of things in our circle of influence and concern. Still yet, at times it is hard to tell by our actions. In all fairness, I'm confident that when an individual says they care about something, that they are being sincere for the most part. However, if our actions do not show caring, then our words are little more than hot air.

The real measure of caring for anything is defined by how we behave in relation to it. This is about to be a huge leap here from the micro-caring sphere to the macro-caring realm, but I promise that one has everything to do with the other. Remember the Iroquois tribe saying. "In our every deliberation, we must consider the impact of our decision on the next seven generations." That is to say that caring in the little means caring in the much. If we are serious about caring for our family, friends, even each other, we owe just consideration to the things that sustains us all. Sure, I want my son to care enough about his public presentation not to disrespect his elders. Even more than that, not to embarrass us all with behavior that is contradictory to what he was taught. But what I would like more than his consciousness in simply caring for the personal things that are closest to him, is a conscious effort to care for everything he has dominion or influence over.

That means caring not only about his elder family members, but all people with whom he comes in contact, his community and country, and, on a larger scale, the world as a whole. Where does caring like that start? There are people starving in countries thousands of miles away. Others are ravaged by natural disasters at any given time, while still others are rife with civil wars or merciless dictators reigning mayhem on their own people. How can I care about any one of those things too great for me to change? I'm not going to pretend that any one of us has the resources or power to do much in affecting great change to issues and challenges as great as any of the ones I just named. However, if we don't care enough to do anything, I can assure you they will not get better on their own.

For us to show a level of caring about macro issues is to do our part on a very small scale. When each of us does what we can on a small scale, those little things add up. I was taking an environmental biology class in completing my Associates degree when I was introduced to the concept of "affluenza." It is the practice by which people of affluence consume in wasteful excess, almost so much so, that it is to the detriment of non-affluent societies. The textbook comparison was that of the developed world in contrast to the developing world. The book stated one statistic which said if every country consumed as much as the United States did, it would take seven planet earths to sustain human life. Look out China, it seems like we're headed for destruction.

The shocking reality to me at that point was that in order for me to live the way I am, someone else has to live impoverished. Anyone who knows me well will attest to the fact that I have never been one to overconsume. I have tried to stay within the realm of necessity and maybe a little extra for comfort's sake. I am one of those people who doesn't believe in taking more food than I'm going to eat. If there is an abundance, then find someone to share it with, and if there is a way to reuse an item, then do it. YES—I recycle! To me that is the first way to contribute to the macro environment in terms of caring.

Consider this, if the raw materials and natural resource usage of the U.S. would be seven earths if the rest of the world combined used the same, what will it look like when just half of China's population is in a position to consume materially just as much as we? The thought is frightening. The answer is clear, either we in the developed world have to be more forward thinking and pre-emptive or more will have to suffer in poverty, disease, and death for us to keep this up. It seems so simple when you think about it. Recycle paper, plastics, and metals. Consume food and other items in necessity and not in excess. Think just as much about tomorrow as you do about today and maybe we can slow down the effects of the desolation of our planet.

I know it doesn't seem like it will help a starving child in Africa, or a tsunami victim in Japan or the Philippines, but every little contribution counts. Besides, if we're honest about caring for our parents, children, friends, and associates, then it would stand to reason that we want them and their lineage to enjoy this world as much as we have. If we continue to pollute our lakes and rivers for profit and consumption, what will happen? If we don't reuse what we can, will there be anything available for those behind us? Should caring only be relegated to the things in your immediate space? If we don't think about the big impact the very little things have on us, and will have on us in the future, we are surely destined for doom.

There is so much that can be said of the importance of caring. Suffice it to say that the most important element of caring is deliberateness. Being aware of interpersonal communication and attentiveness to the intricacies of how it's done. Keeping in mind that certain media doesn't provide all the necessary means to completely get our point across. If we really care, we will do our little part to show that we do in our contribution. Above all, caring is about consideration. If you care, you don't have to say so because your actions will say loud and clear that you do.

FRIENDSHIP

The great thing about friends is that we get to choose them. A friend is a person that you meet at some point in your life that you grow close to and eventually develop a bond with. In many ways, a friend becomes a part of your family, like extended family members. A friend is a person with whom you usually share many things in common and before long you grow to love. You will come across numerous people with whom you will associate, but a true friend is a one in a million occurrence.

Our friends are the people who shape and mold our image of the reality we live. They are the people who we allow close enough to us to either hurt us or build us up. Their input is invaluable because it means just enough to us that it can affect how we behave. A friend, for better or worse, is one of the few people that can have a powerful impact on your life.

One of the most valuable and powerful things to be said of friendship is that just because you are someone's friend, that does not necessarily make them yours. People are communal by nature (some of us more than other), and for the most part, we all need company at some point or another. Therefore, it's natural to desire that most of your interpersonal relationships have a reciprocating factor of mutual camaraderie. As with every other part of behavioral characteristics, the way a person perceives, and values friendship will depend on what is important to them. The best thing about friendship is that it usually starts because the two people share a number of common interests. Therefore, it is more likely that the people we choose as friends will value many of the same things that we do, with a little room for unique personal differences.

Even so, there may come a time when the situation presents itself that we have been a friend to another and have not been treated well in return. There is no easy fix in a situation like this. It will not feel good to have given someone intimate access to yourself only to find out that that person does not share the same value or sentiment for the relationship as you do. These kinds of situations are the character building experiences that stretch us to be ready and able to deal with other relationship challenges in our lesser personal interactions. In those times, we have to question whether our relationship with this person is a healthy one that is indicative of self-respect and self-love.

Once you have decided whether the relationship is worth continuing or ending, you should proceed accordingly. If you decide to remain associated with the person, it will be critical to set healthy boundaries inside which you engage the person and relationship. It is possible to maintain a personal relationship with someone who does not exactly reciprocate the same level of admiration and respect for the relationship as you do. This is the process of being a friend from a distance.

The friends you do get during a lifetime will be few and far between. Many of your associates will appear at first like friends. Time will tell if they are or not. Those who are will stick around. Those who aren't will sooner than later fall by the wayside. One quality in determining if someone is a friend or foe is analyzing if they have your best interest at heart.

Life is a growing and learning process in which our friends will play a huge part. Like actors in a motion picture our friends are the characters that set the stage and create the drama of our lives. We learn together. Not every lesson is always pleasant, but most are necessary to develop our character. It is how we behave in those instances that says whether a person is a friend or not. Provided you can definitively say the person has given you real consideration, that relationship has the qualities necessary for friendship.

With those that do not have your best interest at heart, nor you theirs, no friendship exists. People who are in and out of your life for one reason or another are in no way your friend. The best way to describe them is as fair-weather friends. When everything is bright and sunny, they're there to enjoy it with you, but when the times get hard they are nowhere to be found. I can speak on their type from experience. Incarceration was a firm test of who was a real friend and who was fair-weather. Before that period in my life, I could call any number of people who were available to do whatever I needed. During and after that time, even real friends were in short supply. To be honest, if a friend meant as little as checking on someone once every blue moon, but consistently—I'd have a big zero in the friend column. There has not been one who I knew before that experience who has consistently during the whole thirteen years reached out to check my pulse and see that I was still alive. I would have lost faith in friendship except that I met one on that journey who has helped me still believe that friends are still real, and friendship is not a posse institution. Thanks, Frank West, Jr.

I've always tried to live by the principle that you should not behave a certain way just because of what someone or another does to you. I've tried to be the individual that treats others the way I want to be treated. Therefore, although my associates that I once called friends have not cared for our relationship in a way that I believe values and signifies friendship, I will not do the same. I believe that a real friend is a friend for a lifetime in spite of what circumstances may develop over the course of time. My friendship is like my love unconditional. I will not let the nature of the circumstances surrounding our relationship determine the outcome. If any friendship that I have ever had is lost, it will not be because I threw it away. I wish always to be the one in a million friend to the friends in my life.

To be that person takes a willingness to be understanding, forgiving, and compromising. It takes an uncanny ability to stand in the other person's shoes and look at the relationship from their point of view. It is a practice that I have employed to great results. I will continue in the way of employing these same principles. As you go about establishing and developing your friendships, it is wise to consider all the things you value about relationships. It will be those things, which are consistent with your values, that will be the bonding agent in your relationships and friendships. It is wise to choose friends who share your values. If you don't, you may find yourself in a parasitic relationship where you give all the love and get nothing in return.

I can speak with some level of certainty about friendships that are one-way streets. As I said before, incarceration has really been a defining factor in the tightness of many of my friendship bonds. To choose to still want to be a friend to the many who have not shown an interest in my well-being has taken much emotional maturity, almost to the point of self-inflicted emotional wounds. At times, it has felt like I was abusing myself by continuing to give consideration to relationships that don't seemingly care about me. Then I'm reminded that my own values for people and relationships won't allow me to just abandon a person because they have not shown an interest or consideration for our relationship.

Sure, we have different views on how we value friendships. I have accepted that I may be forced to love them from a distance from this point forward. I understand that in order not to be emotionally disturbed by the conditions of those relationships, I have chosen to not internalize the hurt that accompanies the feeling of abandonment. The only way to stay true to the position of unconditional love, adoration, and admiration for the relationship is to see the person and relationship from unemotional eyes.

If terminating the relationship becomes absolutely necessary, which may occur— then you must do what needs to be done. Before you do, make sure you have done all in your power to salvage the friendship. Then, when it's clear that nothing more can be done, it's alright to let go. In fact, sometimes letting go may be the best thing. Especially when a relationship is toxic and unhealthy for both the parties involved. A real friend is one who wants to see the best for his friend. Even if that means letting them go so they can grow without you.

If you remember nothing else about friendship, remember this; in a lifetime you will not get more than a few. Possibly enough to count on two hands, but more than likely one hand will be enough. Cherish those people. They will be responsible for some of your life's greatest joys and memories. They will also be responsible for some of your life's greatest sorrows and tragedies. All this will grow you into either a person of destination or hostility and embitterment. Ultimately, you have the power to decide how you internalize those experiences. You can be weighted down and burdened by the challenges you experience in your friendships or you can use them to motivate and empower you to be a better person after you've risen to overcome a challenge.

Lastly, friendship extends beyond those you establish with your peers and people you meet. Each relationship you establish has an element of friendship within it. Parent/child, teacher/student, mentor/mentee and the like all have an element of friendship within them. A lot of times we miss the friendship quality of some of our other relationships because we confine them to the established bases that we know them to be. We miss opportunities to share intimate details with people we love because we are following pre-conditions set by others on how those relationships work.

For example, my mother, father, and grandmothers on both sides all share a friendship well beyond the traditional like none other. By sharing a friendship with these people beyond the traditional role, I've been able to learn so much more, share so much more, and live so much more and all without the fear of violating any of the traditional confines of the respect for the status of age. I did not have that same kind of experience with any of my great grandfathers or grandfathers. This is a condition that I don't want to repeat with my own boys.

That's why I have always attempted to engage my boys on both levels. Distinctively setting the boundaries of our traditional relationship, then identifying the area of our relationship where our friendship dwells. There is the conversation that we must have to give them the correct guidance and input in order to make the best choices. We must also have the conversations that are candid, the real-life nitty-gritty on the world and about life unlike the lessons my parents never taught. These are the ones I had to learn on my own from first-hand experience.

I believe the more information with which you are armed the better prepared you'll be to handle life as it happens. Friendships are arguably the most influential interactions we have in our lives. What good does it do to be in a one-sided relationship where I pour into them other things that are not applicable in their real lives. If we have an open and honest friendship, they should feel that they are able to talk to me without fear. If we have that type of rapport in our relationship, they are liberated to share everything without concern about being judged. That type of openness will help me give them the best direction I can as long as they're willing to share.

Hopefully, if our relationship has not developed into one where a friendship of this magnitude exists, this will serve as an invitation to begin one. As they've grown up with someone, they consider to be a good friend, I would hope that as we grow they will consider me equally the same.

FAMILY

Family is the blessing and curse that, unlike your friends, you don't get to choose. Hence, the curse in the whole equation. The blessing of family is that in many ways they are responsible for creating much of the person we develop into. Our family is the closest thing to us in the first stages of life that influences and shapes who we are and how we see life.

On occasion, they are even responsible for many of the hardships we endure. For instance, if a child is given up for adoption it would be the fault of the biological parents that the child would have to grow up in conditions that may prove challenging in the long run. Even if the child is adopted into a wonderful home by great adoptive parents, they may still struggle with the emotional void and disconnect of not knowing their biological parents. The idea here is to keep in mind that your family is not a choice you get to make and what you have is what you get.

That being the case, we must learn to deal with our circumstances and use them to help propel us to the next level. All things considered; I believe I was blessed beyond measure to have been born into the family I was. On both sides, I had great grandparents, grandparents, parents, a stepfather, and a slew of aunts, uncles, and cousins. I was fortunate enough to have a personal relationship with most of them. Their input was critical to the person I am today. It was a combination of character traits that I saw and appreciated from every one of them that I internalized and used to create my own system of morals and values.

Likewise, there were many things I saw on the way that I didn't much care for. In those instances, I developed a strong resolve not to emulate those traits. Overall, it is the gift of family that gave me the necessary tools to go out in the world and make decisions, right and wrong, in my development process. The hierarchical structure helped me to know and understand respect for authority. The peer level relationships helped me get a healthy sense of competition and shape the idea of sharing. The interaction between the younger ones and myself showed me what responsibility was all about. The numerous other interactions between the family unit, the outside world, and me demonstrated everything else.

Since family is the gift nobody asks for, the most crucial thing in our family life we can do is master our relationships for achieving the maximum benefit from them. It would do us good to love, honor, respect and protect our family. Having lived long enough, I can confidently say I know that may not always be the easiest thing to do. Because our immediate family is so close to us, under the same roof, with the extended family never too far away, they are the very people who have endless opportunities to rub us the wrong way. As a matter of fact, they are the very people who, more often than not, provide us with the greatest challenges of our lives. Sibling rivalry, overbearing authoritarian parents, nosy aunts, competitive cousins, and others can all be enough to drive a person mad.

The challenge in these cases is to find the silver lining in the storm cloud. I'm sometimes saddened when I hear people talk about their family in unkind terms. Many times, if you listen long enough, you find they have good reason for feeling the way they do. However, the disheartening part of the whole equation is that you only get one family and a very short life to enjoy them in. It is a shame when we get so caught up in minute situational circumstances that we refuse to enjoy our family as much as we can for the brief period, we have each other. Granted, if the situation is beyond your control and you're powerless to affect change, that is the time when you must be willing to live with the reality. It is just a great loss not to be able to capitalize on the wonderful experiences that family provides.

I am not at all suggesting that a person allow another who is abusive to them in any capacity to influence or affect them just because they are family or that you should tolerate a person's behavior if it violates your principles. I am just encouraging you to set aside minor differences and enjoy each other in some capacity before it's too late. I said minor differences. I would not suggest that a person who has a drug addicted sibling enable their habit. A child that has a verbally abusive parent should not subject themselves to verbal abuse simply out of respect for their elders. A child who doesn't agree with their parent's moral or social beliefs is not expected to continue in that behavior provided it is something that is not in line with what's correct.

There are several individuals in my own family who do things that I don't like. In fact, there are those who do things that are downright offensive, to be honest. In order to not air out any of our dirty laundry, I'll elect to not use anyone else as an example. The truth can be a very ugly thing to have to confront; therefore, to keep it simple, I'll use myself and some of my own ugliness to highlight examples of tolerance and acceptance with limitations. The goal is to enjoy your family while you have them. We simply never know when they'll be gone.

When I was going through my growing pains, I gave my mother and father much grief. By ages 14 and 15, I was in the streets all times of the night. Sometimes I would stay gone for days on end. I was smoking, drinking, doing drugs, selling drugs, stealing cars, playing with guns, and a bunch of other reckless behavior that, if documented, Allstate would refuse to provide life insurance coverage.

Neither of my parents condoned this kind of behavior, and I wasn't smart enough to be discreet about my actions. I didn't overtly announce, "Look Mom, I got a gun and drugs," but I didn't exactly hide it either. In hindsight, I see now how foolish and reckless my behavior was; however, it was hard at that age to make the association between what was wrong and what I was doing.

Needless to say, my parents did not condone or appreciate my behavior. A number of times when they were frustrated and at a loss for what to do, they would throw their hands up and seemingly give up, only to catch their second wind and jump back in to go a few more rounds with me. They never gave up completely. They would continue to try to expose me to the things they felt I would need in the future. When my mother would call frustrated about something I'd done, my grandmother would tell her, "You can't throw the baby out with the bath water." I'm sure this helped immensely in bringing her back to a center point of tolerance. Alternately, I've seen my father over the years dissolve several intimate relationships. At the same time, he's written me out of the will a few times in the past, but unlike those other relationships that never repaired themselves, ours has always managed to be reconciled.

Examples in our own relationships have been enough for me to develop a sense of how invaluable acceptance, tolerance, forgiveness, and compromise are with family. Our interactions were the early lessons that gave me the backdrop to be able to deal with the rest of my family accordingly, and then, later, with my own children, the same. The lesson of allowing a person the space needed to grow was conveyed loud and clear. Another memorable lesson was to never stop providing the essentials, even when the recipient is not receptive. And, as an adult, I now know how unbelievably frustrating that can be. One of the most important lessons I think I learned in all that was the value of accepting a person for who, what and how they are. We learned to compromise on common grounds so we can enjoy each other without the resistance or hostility because of our different value systems colliding.

These are the invaluable lessons that our families will provide us with if we are open to receiving them. They will extend to cover our entire family if we look for every opportunity to internalize the good and beneficial lessons in every experience good and bad. The reality is there are no good or bad experiences; only the results of the positive or negative of how we internalize them. It's like a person who grows up in a negative environment who uses the discomfort of their situation to motivate them to achieve and succeed beyond the condition that burdens them. On the outside, we can say they came from a bad situation to make something good—the reality is that it was that situation that was the motivating factor that helped propel them to their place of success and prosperity.

If you can attribute all your success to the conditions of your environment, which on the surface appeared bad, I'm sure you would ultimately consider it the best thing that ever happened to you; so it is with our family experiences. By looking for the silver lining in every storm cloud, we are able to take positive and negative stimuli and process them into motivating elements that are going to be healthy and beneficial for us throughout our lifetime. There are numerous examples of people who seem to have had it all but somehow end up in an unhealthy situation down the line. Look at Britney Spears, Lindsay Lohan, Miley Cyrus, and Michael Jackson. These people have or had all the material success and fame anyone could ever want; however, they have all suffered some very shameful public embarrassments.

In the alternative, there is a book called "*The Pact*" by medical doctors Sampson Davis, George Jenkins, and Rameck Hunt who grew up in Newark, New Jersey, who were all fatherless and overcame some pretty challenging odds to achieve their success. They are just three of many who have used their circumstances and family situations to motivate them to achieve great success. There are numerous other examples of people just like them who chose to take the negative stimuli and create a better physical reality. Each of us will have the choice in how we allow that situation to weigh on us.

All things considered, our family is the staging ground for the coming challenges and rigors of life. If we are fortunate, we will get all the necessary elements in order to be healthy, happy, and productive. There are occasions when we don't have those elements immediately in our reach, but it is hard to live your whole life without coming into contact with them, as necessary elements, at some point. A concerned teacher, a friend's parents, a loving aunt or uncle, youth athletics' coach, a leader in some youth organization—somewhere along the line we come across positive influences that can help guide us in a better direction. The question then becomes whether we will take the advice and direction. The choice is always our own.

Perhaps as a youth, if you were anything like me myself, you missed the message a time or two. Maybe you even rejected the counsel and lost the opportunity to use the family structure and the early years as a preparatory period. The great part about it is, if you are not dead, the opportunity for improvement still exists. Under the most sublime conditions, like my own, you will have held onto many of those early instructions, which in turn will mean that the early staging ground lessons were not a total loss. At the point of awareness, whether it's early on or even while reading this book, you can always start to get it together from that point on.

There is a conversation that I often have with my youngest son when he complains of having had a less than ideal home environment very early on. As he neared legal adulthood somewhere around fifteen, I would say to him that though his situation was less than perfect because of everyone else's doing, mainly his mother's and mine, that his future conditions would be at the hands of his own doing.

The kid is one hell of a trooper. At two he was forced to come live with me because his mother was single handily attempting to raise him and three others. A devastating circumstance for a toddler, I'm sure, for not knowing why you cannot be with your siblings at a time when the love, support, and fellowship of the pack is critical. I cannot count the number of nights he cried on my stomach after talking to his mom and siblings questioning why he had to stay with me by himself and couldn't be with them. Each time I would hug him, holding him until he was comforted and reassure him that they all loved him and it was just temporary until things got better, and he would be able to return. I tried as best I could, but I'm almost certain it did not clearly register what was really going on in his two-year-old mind.

Then, as if he didn't have enough to deal with from his early challenges, I did not make it any better. When he was six, I was arrested for a probation violation and incarcerated six months. He was bounced from my house to my mother's in the middle of a school year, uprooted and thrust into a new neighborhood, home, and school. I came back for a brief fifteen months while I waited to be convicted for an offense that would take me from him for the next thirteen years. I'll never forget the day. I sat him, his older brother, and my little brother down and explained that I would be leaving them for more than a decade. They were ten, eight, and six. Still, to this day, I feel the experience of that abandonment as being the greatest sin I ever committed.

Sometime after I had been gone for a year, maybe two, he went back to live with his mother. She had more space and could accommodate him, but it was worlds away from the conditions that I or my mother had provided for him. First, there were at least five of them and sharing was a must. Then, the neighborhood was less desirable in comparison, so was the school, and so on and so on. These were all circumstances that were beyond his control.

All of them were at the hands of his mother or me. In fact, I fault myself the most in the whole equation because, regardless of what she did, I should have been there to take care of the home. That is the way my mother reared me. One of her most memorable admonishments to me was that as a man I better be ready to take care of my children when I have them, so, in actuality, I am the most culpable for the majority of his circumstances.

That is why I feel it so important to have this conversation with him. To express the fact that he can do one of two things, allow his situation to either create a defeatist mentality or to be the motivation to keep him trying to improve himself for getting beyond his current condition. He can embody the defeatist mentality and say to himself, "It's my parents fault that I am this way, and I can never get beyond what I see being what I get," or, he can say to himself, "I hate these conditions and I do not want to stay here, and I will do all in my power to rise up out of this condition." Either way, the choice is completely his. All I know is he is extremely strong to have endured what he has thus far. I'm fully confident that he will find the strength and determination necessary to convert what was seemingly negative input into the motivating fuel of success. I am 100 percent certain that if and when he decides to head in that direction, he will have 100 percent of my energy and resources at his disposal for him to get there.

The family structure is one that no matter how discomforting, dysfunctional, and burdensome it is—it's one to which we are obligated, nonetheless. Similar to when I did things to both of my parents that violated their principles and what they would tolerate, I was still their child all the same. Equally so, in my son's case, his mother and I will always be his parents regardless of the mental and emotional distress we've caused him.

With that in mind, it does us good to find the path of least resistance in our interactions with our families. Almost always that means taking the road less traveled when we find ourselves in challenging situations. Because we love our family so much, it is even more difficult to take the moral high ground in many of the interactions we have with them.

Dr. Stephen Covey wrote in the *Seven Habits of Highly Effective People* "to seek first to understand and then to be understood." This is a practice that I found works extremely well when dealing with anyone, but with family especially. In our family, we exchange so many emotional transactions that they often weigh heavier on our psyche than those outside the family unit. Imagine the weight of feeling like a parent doesn't love you because they are absent from your life for some reason. Or how about the dysfunction of dealing with the drug addiction of a sibling? Maybe they steal from you or get high and are abusive. These types of things can devastate a person; however, if we seek first to understand, it can help make us more empathetic to their circumstances and position. It will not

84

remedy the effects of the conditions, but it can minimize the turmoil that can be caused by dysfunctional behavior.

Mostly, family requires unconditional love with limits. It sounds like an oxymoron. Unconditional love means love without limits. However, in the case of family, it may mean that you set necessary boundaries in order to keep the relationship healthy and progressive. This creates a condition where unconditional love can manifest and grow. In "*The Pact*," one of the doctors spoke about his siblings being his idols and how their behavior, which was largely a negative influence, shaped the way he viewed the world around him. He went on to say that as he went onto excel to new heights that he had to make hard choices about his family conditions and put limitations on those relationships in order to get where he was going.

I don't think the conditions of his love had changed for them so much as his environmental conditions had changed forcing him to make some choices about what was most important. Our family is a debt that we must serve at varying times in our development in any number of ways. Parents must take care of children, siblings are responsible for a certain level of influence and direction on each other. There are occasions when negative stimuli must be transferred into usable measuring tools and motivating fuel for improvement and achievement. All told, family is an establishment of unconditional love that must be mastered and contained inside of healthy boundaries that will help us to be productive and successful people.

In the end, all we have is us. When no other friends exist, when the community has turned its back on us, when our romantic relationships fail, when we are sick or any serious tragedy befalls us, our family is whom we have to fall back on for support. It behooves us to be attentive to the proper development of our family unit. If we have been careful and deliberate in building a strong and stable family unit, it should serve us well for a lifetime. It will also be the undergirding factor in a strong and healthy family for generations to come. After all, we generally pass on what we know and are taught—good and bad.

HUSBANDHOOD

Husbandhood is a family status that changes the dynamics of the family structure permanently. Before marriage, men usually give a number of other things high priority in their family structure. A single man with no children may typically hold the elder women, mom, grandmothers and others in high esteem. Those of us who have children before marriage will generally hold our children in fairly high regard of importance—and if we don't, we should. Then somewhere around the serious girlfriend and the fiancée, we tend to shift the priority of our relationship status of importance from those other things to our romantic relationship.

Husbandhood should be your first real intimate, romantic experience, the precursor of which should be all your dating experiences leading up to that one relationship that you believe is the one, the one to which you believe is worth committing your whole self for the rest of your life. When we examine the spiritual, not religious, side of our romantic relationship, we are better able to understand the premise of matrimony being the ultimate union between man and woman creating one body or person. All our intimate encounters preceding that one is all growing experiences along the way there. When we join ourselves to a woman, we essentially become one with that person. That ideology is what usually causes us to put that relationship above all others.

The woman you choose, and you will together be responsible for caring for the family that you create and the ones that you have brought with you to the union. That is why it is so important to be conscious of taking perfect care of that relationship first, caring for it with the same level of consideration, attention, and love that we give ourselves. It is an absolute fact that if we are not fulfilled in our romantic relationship with our significant other, we will be unbalanced and lacking in the rest of our relationships. That's why we should pay great attention to our woman because she will likely be the determining factor in what level of success we will ultimately achieve.

For some of us, our cultural norms have not been full of good examples of the marriage bond, fidelity and husbandhood. Sadly, many of the examples with the most powerful influence on us are stereotypical and negative in consideration of meaningful examples of healthy relationships. Without good examples throughout the development process, we are ill-prepared to be good and fit husbands even if we make it that far in a relationship with a woman.

For young minority men, blacks especially, the early examples of absentee fathers, mothers, who are in and out of romantic relationships with numerous partners, and a number of other elements makes it hard to recognize what a healthy intimate relationship between the sexes looks like. There are the influences of pop culture, displays of either partner in various and numerous romantic relationships (men especially), the not so discreet messages in music, the over-sexualization of women on TV, videos, and movies, and the common undertone of your peer group about boyfriend-girlfriend relationships that present an unhealthy slant on male-female interactions.

After having been conditioned over a long period of time with unhealthy input on romantic and committed relationships, we can develop a distorted view of what commitment and fidelity are. Speaking from experience, the message that is presented and repeated from a very early age is one of conquest, prowess and bragging rights. In my peer group, it seemed to start around the pubescent shift of between twelve at the earliest, and fourteen the latest when we became intently focused on the opposite sex. Back then the bragging rights were more modest in that kissing, touching prohibited body parts, and talking dirty to little girls were enough to say you had done something.

It wasn't long after fourteen that those rights would be challenged by more advanced acts of intimacy. In my era, if you were a fourteen-year-old virgin you were the laughingstock of your peer group. That is when conquest began to take shape. Needless to say, I don't remember anyone in our peer group who stood out from the rest by abstaining from sexual acts. No one wanted to seem slow-to-go; therefore, both boys and girls in our group of friends each made sure to lose their virginity in a socially acceptable timeframe.

I wish I could say that there were other elements around us speaking a message of abstinence. There were safe sex campaigns because we grew up in the HIV/AIDS era, but other media, like music, videos, TV and movies seemed to encourage sexual promiscuity. Couple that with poor examples in the community and peer pressure and you have a situation unideal for creating a good environment for making future husbands.

One very influential element that aids in creating a faulty perception of intimate relationships is music. It is unfair to cast a blanket indictment of musicians and music for the dysfunctional nature of commitment in intimate relationships, but, if we're honest, we have to give it due consideration. The message in a lot of music in recent years has promoted promiscuity, infidelity, selfishness and a number of other unhealthy elements. Combined with the imagery that is displayed in the videos, there is an overwhelming amount of negative stimuli being pushed at us from all different angles. Without any other forces feeding us better messages and examples, it becomes easy for us to get caught up in the hype. Moreover, it makes it that much more challenging for us to identify correct behavior. This happens even in instances when we have access to models of better behavior.

The worst part of it all is that even if and when we are able to identify that we have a faulty perception of commitment and intimate relationships we have become so stuck in our dysfunction that we resist change. I know because I deal with the issue of a faulty mentality on commitment and intimacy every day. I wish I could say that shortly after adolescence in our early adulthood we grow out of the childish mentality of sexual prowess, multiple lovers, and emotional disconnection or withholding. More likely than not, we continue to think that behavior like this is ok, and, subsequently, it becomes our norm.

It takes a very conscious effort to identify the fault in this perception and recalibrate and make the necessary adjustments to go in a better direction in your personal relationships. In order to enter the union of marriage with the slightest chances of success, we have to take a long hard look at our ideals in regard to committed and intimate relationships. There are a number of things that need to be addressed in our thinking before we should consider making a commitment as meaningful as is marriage. If we fail to address these critical elements it is just about certain that any efforts at maintaining an intimate and committed relationship will fail.

First is the male tendency to want more than one woman. If there is any part of you that is still desirous of playing the field, then it would do you good to postpone committing to a serious relationship with one woman. It is also advisable to be honest with the woman with whom you decide to have intimate interactions that you are not ready to settle down. For most of us, that doesn't come naturally or easy—telling women in potential mating situations that we are not looking for an exclusive relationship; however, it is the best gift you can give a woman—choice. It is a noble thing to do to give the woman the choice of getting intimately and emotionally involved with you on her own terms. This way, at the end of the day, she can, at the very least, say that the position in which she finds herself was by her own doing.

If you manage to settle on one woman, you will be tasked with the challenge of being monogamous. A lot of times we think that because we are not dating more than one woman, we're being faithful. We mistakenly think that the occasional venturing away from the home front for a quick physical encounter with another woman is alright and meaningless. Besides, it is in our nature to want more than one woman and a socially acceptable norm amongst our peer group. Some of us have been doing this all our lives and don't see anything wrong with the behavior. The problem is that infidelity, once identified by your partner, will cause a lack of trust and confidence in the relationship to develop in them. It also leads to other issues like possible disease transmission to your partner.

A lack of trust and confidence will cause the relationship to deteriorate over time. To counter the effects that a misappropriation of either will cause, it is a best practice to attempt to be sexually monogamous. If you don't believe yourself capable of monogamy, then you should again tell your partner and allow them the option of continuing to maintain a relationship with you in an intimate capacity. One thing you will be able to accomplish by doing so is a level of mutual respect that will encourage honesty and promote openness. With those two things in a relationship, you are on better grounds to communicate the important issues that will come down the line.

Considering we are able to master ourselves to the point of commitment and monogamy which is a constant balancing act, we can focus on other important things needed to make matrimony work. There are several elements that are essential to making a marriage work: willingness to listen, consideration, understanding, compromise, selflessness, and a whole lot of love, in no particular order of importance. A good, even distribution of all these elements are actually necessary to achieve cohesiveness in the marriage bond.

As men, we are challenged with the responsibility of leadership in the family structure. Being a good and effective leader requires us to model certain characteristics that are indicative of the type of atmosphere whereby the afore-mentioned elements can take flight and grow. One main characteristic that will go a long way in the marriage arrangement is the ability to listen to our spouse. By listening earnestly and trying to understand what our partner is trying to tell us, we create an environment whereby things like compromise and consideration are that much easier. If we fail to listen to the concerns of our other half, we create a very unbalanced atmosphere that is ripe for dysfunction to develop. Failure to listen also says to others that you are self-absorbed and inconsiderate. This is a poor example to model at any time, but especially in front of children, provided you decide to have them.

Due consideration is another critical element in creating a workable relationship between a husband and wife. To be considerate is to be thoughtful of the other person, their feelings, thoughts, and desires. Men are usually more logic and thought-driven people. Women are more feelings and emotion oriented. What that means for us is that it is imperative that we make extra effort to take our woman's perspective into full consideration when we make decisions that will affect both of us and our family. It is easy for us to get caught up in the macho mentality and become consumed with doing things our way. If we will be patient and receptive to our emotional side, our own "feminine" side, we will often be given the other half of the input we need to make a more balanced and healthy decision for ourselves and our family.

Understanding and compromise go hand in hand. When we have listened to understand and not just answer, given due consideration to the other person, and have found a common ground of workableness that is suitable to all the parties involved, we come to a place of compromise. Why compromise is so important is because it signifies to the other person that they matter to you. For anyone engaged in a committed relationship, the knowledge that your partner cares is uncompromising. It is a must-have element or the relationship cannot survive. Compromise is also a leadership trait that is often overlooked. Essentially compromise means sharing. If you are not able to share at the stage of your life when you are married, or getting married, you have a lot of growing to do.

I used to watch a talk show on the Spanish channel called "Quién Tiene La Razón," which means, "Who's Right?" The host, Dr. Nancy Alvarez, used to have a saying of which I grew fond. She would say, "Para que el amor funciona, amarse no es suficiente." That means, roughly, "For a relationship to work, just love is not enough." Which brings me to the last ingredient in the making of a healthy marriage house. Love is much like what we discussed in the section titled Love. In the marriage bond, it takes on a whole new dynamic. Love is the default mechanism we resort to when the challenges of our life and relationship consume us. It is the common denominator that can help keep us together when circumstances prove more than we can handle mentally or emotionally.

The wisdom in Dr. Alvarez's saying is that, with love and all the other elements we've discussed in this section, there is hope that a marriage can function and prosper. If we are true in our love for our mate, we will find it less challenging to be selfless in our emotional transactions. Combined, all these elements put us in a better position to be good husbands, role models, and leaders. Even if we don't have children of our own, there are people watching us and emulating our actions. Husbandhood is an act of devotion to something greater than yourself. When you unite with a woman, you essentially give up your rights to yourself. You now share those rights with the woman you have chosen.

Husbandhood is an exercise of commitment that causes us to have to submit to our woman just as we expect her to submit to us. Sometimes we get the mistaken idea that because we are the physically dominate sex that we should only dominate and not submit. Nothing could be further from the truth. For

90

example, if your wife admonishes you to eat healthier, stop or cut back on destructive behavior like drinking, abusing drugs or any number of other health hazards, we are obligated to submit to her wise counsel. After all, she has just as much a right to want to enjoy you for as long as she can. If doing these simple things will be a means to that end, we owe it to them.

Practicing the arts of patience, temperance, and prudence are also elements that will serve you well in your husband-wife relationship. Overall, marriage is a union that you will learn as you go. It's just like the toy's packaging that says "Batteries Not Included." No matter how many good books you read on the subject or how far you feel yourself ahead of the game, there's no substitute for the real thing. I ought to know; I got married at twenty-three and was divorced by twenty-five. A very short experience because, at the time, I was not mentally or emotionally prepared for the responsibility. I'm sure in that relationship we each did our fair share of destroying the marriage. When it all boils down, I fault myself because as the man, leader, and head of the relationship, I was the one most responsible for its care and direction.

Now that I am much wiser, I know better how to treat the next relationship I engage, with that level of commitment. I can say this with all certainty that I will never again take the marriage bond lightly. Women give up so much of themselves when they commit to a man in an intimate relationship. It is selfish and inconsiderate not to return to your woman the same level of respect, admiration, and adoration as she gives you. Husbandhood is a constant effort. You will always need to be on point looking for ways to improve your relationship. It is an investment well worth its weight in gold. You will get out of your marriage what you put into it.

FIDELITY & FAITHFULNESS

The Merriam Webster Collegiate Dictionary defines faithfulness as allegiance to duty or a person: loyalty: complete trust. There are other definitions pertaining to the religious significance of the word, but for the moment we are focusing on the meaning as it relates to people and our relationships. It also defines fidelity as the quality or state of being faithful. Which means fidelity is created as a result of one's faithfulness.

Fidelity is a little easier to see and measure in the confines of our romantic relationships. As we grow and experience the growing pains of commitment to another person, we can see clearly the importance of allegiance and duty to another person. The commitment is a recognized agreement between us and the other individual to maintain a certain kind of bond. The bond should include a level of trust and loyalty that assures the other person that you are just as committed to the relationship as they are. In an ideal situation, that is how it would work. Having had the interaction of a romantic relationship to gauge from, you can reasonably define fidelity for yourself.

What happens if we have not had those kind of experiences or examples modeled to us in the past? For those of us who have not had either healthy exchanges with the practice of faithfulness or good examples of the behavior, it becomes a hard sale. In order to value a practice such as fidelity, we need to have had some regular encounters that have given us a halfway decent example of what it looks and feels like.

For too many of us, myself included, the examples, stimuli, and to a certain extent, the cultural norm does not celebrate fidelity and faithfulness. On the contrary, a common undertone in my own peer group from the earliest days, and sadly even today, has been to celebrate multiple partners (especially sex partners) promiscuity and infidelity. As young men, it was more understandable if you factored in the fact that many of us were, as they say, "young, dumb, and full of cum." Without good examples of the practice and multiple sources of media input force feeding us negative imagery to reinforce our already faulty perception, it's more tolerable and understandable when a young man exhibits character flaws marked by infidelity.

However, when that behavior persists into early adulthood and then over a lifetime, it is not only intolerable, but unacceptable as well. If I had to offer a cause that I believe drives this behavior in grown men who should know better,

I'd have to start with conditioning. When we practice a certain behavior for an extended period of time, it becomes ingrained in our mind. The mentality becomes our nature, and as a consequence, we begin to behave in accordance with what feels natural to us. Couple that with other outside stimuli we receive from media like music, TV, and movies, and we can see how we are being constantly fed a mental diet of unhealthy input to respond to. That is neither an excuse nor justification for the behavior; simply a semi-logical possibility for why it exists.

One practice that may do much to help us begin to overcome the mentality that is created as a result of faulty preconditioning is to conquer our intimate relationship first and try to identify the value of fidelity and faithfulness in all relationships. If we have never had a good understanding of faithfulness in our relationships, it is hard to assign a meaningful value to fidelity. It may require that you look to something else that you have pledged your loyalty to and use that as a plumb-line with which to measure.

Maybe it's your mother or your "homies" in your gang, or your child. It can be any relationship that you value enough that you would not want to diminish the confidence and trust factor in. Use that relationship with that outside element and the value you have placed on not jeopardizing it as a point of reference for how you should be treating your romantic commitment.

By conquering our intimate relationship, first we gain more opportunities to practice the behavior. Our romantic relationship is a constant in our lives. Your girlfriend or spouse is 24/7. There are no days off, no time between the next encounter—they are with you at all times. Even in the event you are not physically together, the existence of the commitment is still real. You are always responsible for maintaining your contribution to the relationship and the stability of your faithfulness. By being conscious of maintaining fidelity in our intimate relationship, we create a great environment for practicing a behavior that will serve us well in all our personal and professional relationships.

The regularity of our intimate relationship is the perfect place to readjust the old habit that we may have created over time when we were youthful and maybe didn't know any better. That behavior was developed over the course of time as a result of exposure to poor training, negative inputs and possibly cultural norms. It has been the course of time that has created the habit. Only the course of time practicing new habits can help change the mentality that produces infidelity and unfaithfulness. After you manage to reestablish better precepts on faithfulness and fidelity in your intimate relationship you will begin to build better character traits that will improve your ability to exercise fidelity overall.

Quite naturally that will improve the quality of your intimate relationship, but what it will also do that is not as readily recognizable is improve the quality of all your interpersonal relationships. Faithfulness by definition is allegiance, loyalty and complete trust to a person. When we create these elements in our friendships, professional life, community environment, or any relationship that requires a level of trustworthiness, imagine how much more effective we will be in those exchanges. Most people enjoy some level of confidence that comes with knowing that the people they are connected to have a level of faithfulness to their commitment.

Fidelity is especially useful in business relationships. It's something that we don't give much consideration to in most instances because in our country, there are many large establishments in the business world that have already firmly established their brand and reputation: McDonalds, Nike, Facebook, Apple; the list goes on and on. These business names have already created such a level of fidelity to the consumer that we don't think twice about using their products or services. They are giants in their industries. We just take for granted that they will provide us a certain level of service or quality of product when dealing with them. They have worked hard to establish this level of trust and are committed to providing that same level of service on a regular basis.

By building our capacity to exercise fidelity in our intimate and personal relationships, we are better prepared to apply those same principles to our business and professional relationships. The value of practicing fidelity in all your relationships is that you will increase the quality and maximize the benefits of those associations. Of course, some of us will have to overcome some level of mis-education and bad habits we've developed. The re- education process requires starting with faithfulness in little and then working our way to readiness for faithfulness in much. We first learn how to identify things we value enough to be loyal to and have a sense of obligation to. We then transition that sense of duty from one relationship, to some relationships, eventually to all relationships.

Fidelity is a quality that will carry you the distance in all your relationships. It is a strengthening agent on many other fronts. This helps others to feel confident that you really have their best interest at heart. Without a doubt practicing faithfulness and fidelity in all your doings is a reward like no other. We generally get back the energy in return that we have put out. If you are looking for a bonding agent that has the power to hold your relationship tightly together, fidelity would be a great starting point.

94

FATHERHOOD

The greatest gift in the world any man could receive is fathering a child. Children are a blessing beyond measure. They are a gift of life that you will have the full responsibility of caring for. They do not ask to be brought into the world. They are completely empty vessels that will be filled with ideas that will affect the rest of their lives, based on the things they learn at home from their mother and father. As a young parent, I was not aware how extremely important my input and contribution would be to my boys. Consequently, looking back, I can see that I left a great many things to chance in my attempts to give them all the things I thought they needed.

Because of my own experience with my parents and their influence on my life, I did want to be a part of my children's lives. My mother stressed that when I did actually father a child, I'd better be ready to take care of them. My father, as far back as I can remember, was an active part of my life. Although he and my mother never married, he did take an active role in my life. Both of them smothered me with love and as much attention as working single parents could. That experience created within me an ideology that a normal family structure was possible even if the parents weren't together; that a parent outside the household could share the responsibility of raising the child.

I loved my kids because I was first loved. It was what came naturally. Still, no amount of loving your child is enough to make you a good father. Children don't come with instructions. The only instructions we ever get about life comes from experiences. If we are observant, we can learn a lot about good healthy habits and ways to live our lives from the examples of others (both good and bad). The older you get, the better situated you are in terms of preparedness for the challenges of adulthood and eventually fatherhood. When I had my first child, I lacked both life experience and number of years.

Shentell, the mother of my first child, had our son when we were sixteen, eleven days before my seventeenth birthday. I was in no condition to take care of a child, but my mother, who does not believe in abortion, assured us that we would all take care of this new life. She had always admonished that when I thought I was grown enough to play, that I'd better be man enough to pay. So, with her assurance, we were having a baby. As a young father, I did not really have a good concept of what my role in my little boy's life should be. I thought I needed to buy Pampers, come visit him at his mother's house sometimes or bring him to my mother's sometimes. When I was around him, I should change his diaper—

feed and burp him and play with him a little, and voila—I was a good dad. I started out strong doing all the above for a very short while, maybe four months. As time wore on, I began to fall into a pattern of irresponsibility and those behaviors began to slack of.

Immaturity was a big factor in my lack of involvement in the early days. I could not make the distinction between my personal relationship with Shentell and my responsibility to our child. She never made an unreasonable request of me. In fact, she asked very little of me when our child was a baby. She did not mix our relationship with my relationship with my son. She rarely called for things like diapers and milk. She asked that I contribute financially by paying for the daycare bill, but besides those reasonable expectations, she did not ask much else.

She herself, on the other hand, went back to high school, worked a part-time job, eventually graduated, immediately went to college, worked two jobs while in school, and eventually graduated with a Bachelor's in Psychology; all the while I was going through the process of growing up. My involvement was scattered and unstable at best. I would come around at my leisure and play daddy, then be undependable for months on end. I did not keep a job, so my financial support was sporadic and inconsistent. If I had it, I would pay the daycare bill, but if I didn't, my attitude was, "Oh well, what could I do?"

That behavior continued until I was eighteen, about to turn nineteen. October 8, 1995, I got shot in the back. As a result, I was paralyzed and confined to a wheelchair. My son was almost two years old. My life took an abrupt U-turn at that point. I had to take a hard look at who I was. The reality of my behavior was brought front and center. I was forced to confront the fact that I had been living a very self-centered, selfish, irresponsible, and completely destructive lifestyle. I didn't want to change; I was forced to change. I could no longer avoid my responsibilities like I had been because my new condition would not allow me to. I had to take on a certain amount of responsibility just to stay alive.

During the one month and one week I spent in the hospital recovering from my injury, I took the time to reassess my life. The one thing that resonated most clearly in my mind is that I almost carelessly threw away my own life. That alone was not the great life changing epiphany though. The fact that I had a life that was and would continue to be dependent on me for support and that I was not selfless enough to think about him was what shook my world to the core.

This young life did not ask to be created. His mother and I decided to engage in an act whereby his life was a possibility and the eventual outcome. It was our responsibility to ensure that we give him what was necessary to develop into a whole and healthy person, at which she was doing an outstanding job for a young mother. It was never so clear to me just how horribly wrong I had gotten my first attempt at fatherhood until Shentell brought my son to visit me in the rehab hospital and he was afraid to come to me. It was then and there that I knew that I had a great deal of work to do in terms of being a good parent.

That interaction was miles away from the ideal relationship that I had daydreamed about in times past. I had been so preoccupied with doing the things that teenage boys usually do that I had missed the signs that I was not being a good parent—well, truthfully not being a parent at all. That experience was a wake-up call. I didn't know what exactly I needed to do to improve the relationship, but I did know that the way our current relationship was, was not the way I wanted our relationship to be. It would be a slow process of reestablishing a better bond between my son and myself, but a necessary process that I was committed to making happen.

In my new physical condition with little to no professional skills, I was ill prepared to make a financial contribution. I had to move back home with my mother so I could readjust to my new condition and figure out a new game plan. Eventually, I got Supplemental Social Security Income benefits (SSI) and subsidized housing. I began to live independently in my new condition. I didn't have much material support to contribute, but I did have time. I could help Shentell with childcare. Assistance she was all too glad to have considering her hectic lifestyle of work and school. As time progressed, I began to be able to make more regular and consistent contributions. Thankfully, Shentell was willing to allow me the space to come along a little late in the game and pick up my slack as if I had never been gone.

Although I'd like to pretend I was a good father from the very first day I found out my girlfriend, Shentell, was pregnant, I would be lying. It was a process of many mistakes before I became remotely aware of the very minimum, I should be doing. Even after I became more involved, I still was not a good parent. I'd say, if I had to grade myself, since I was around and barely doing anything, my grade would just be a "D." There was so much more to fatherhood that I would learn as I went through the experience. This was too late in the grand scheme of parenthood and raising healthy, balanced, and happy boys to men.

Fatherhood is one of the biggest obligations of a lifetime. Our children will learn responsibility/irresponsibility, morals/values or lack thereof, love and compassion, integrity and a host of other character traits by what we teach them very early in their lives. We are the first examples they are exposed to. It is our responsibility to correct behavior that is contrary to good, strong character traits that will serve them well throughout a lifetime. To simply give a child affection is not enough. It is important to ensure they have the necessary skills to make it in this very cruel and sometimes vicious world. Although love is an integral ingredient in a well-balanced individual's development, life skills are essential tools that every child needs in order to have a positive and productive life.

My father was very affectionate with me. He was always hugging me, kissing me, and telling me he loved me at every opportunity he got. I found it easy, in fact natural, to do the same thing with my own children. Some of my peers have shared with me that they don't remember their fathers ever telling them they loved them. Between men, it is not a regular or celebrated practice to kiss or hug. Therefore, often men don't hug or kiss their sons. These things are essential in sharing the love message. Nothing says "I love you" like a hug and kiss. Especially in the early years.

As we grow, we tend to outgrow the condition of wanting to be hugged and kissed as much as we did as little boys. Something about gender roles in our society makes it un-cool for men to exchange hugs and kisses. At some point, if we had hugged and kissed our male children, we would stop because it is no longer socially acceptable. All these elements contribute to the fact that men do not share more intimate exchanges on a regular basis. They are mentalities and conditions that we must change and overcome if we are to employ one critical necessity in giving our sons the things they need to become better men.

Provided we are able to overcome the need for the social approval of the outside world about how we interact with our children, we are better situated to give them the other tools and skills they need. Because your duty as a father is a debt that you are responsible for, you are charged with the responsibility of making some major sacrifices. Your time is no longer your own. It now belongs to the child in equal amounts. The things that you were able to do when you didn't have the responsibility of a child are no longer appropriate now that you are a father.

Your relationship with their mother is crucial. Especially for those of us who choose not to stay together after the child is born. It is important not to use the child as a pawn in the relationship. If the romantic relationship is broken and dysfunctional, it is alright to walk away from it. It is not okay to walk away from the responsibility of caring for the child.

Far too many times, guys use the baby as a ticket back between the mother's legs at their convenience. There are just as many instances when women do the same, using the child against the father. However, this discourse is about manhood and what the defining characteristics of manhood are; therefore, the focal point is our responsibility as men. Life will present us all types of adverse circumstances that we cannot do anything about. A woman using a child to hurt a man may be one of them, but we can only be responsible for how we react and what we do.

If you find yourself in a situation that the mother of your child is being disagreeable and unaccommodating—you are still responsible for doing your part at whatever the cost may be to you in personal sacrifice. My mother gave it to me best at a time when I was struggling with my second child's mother about her unwillingness to allow me to be a part of our child's life. She said, "Son, time has a way of working all things out for the man who is patient enough to endure the challenges." I didn't fully understand the significance at the time, but I took what she said to mean "Be patient and things will get better." They did.

After having made so many mistakes with my first son in terms of my involvement, I did not want to repeat the same mistakes with the second. I wanted to be physically, financially, mentally, and emotionally involved. Only my second son's mother, Elsa, was not as accommodating as the first. She had already gotten involved in another intimate relationship with a man. Interacting with me, her ex, was not an ideal situation to be in if she hoped to keep her current relationship together and drama free. I did not mind her desire to limit our contact in order to help her relationship thrive. I considered that a reasonable want; however, preventing me from having any contact with the child was disturbing.

Because of that situation, I did not get to see my second son until he was nine months old. Elsa first told me she was pregnant in the summer of 1995. The message came with the disclaimer that she was not 100 percent sure the child she was carrying was mine. She and I were between relationships and still fooling around on occasion and she got pregnant right before meeting the guy with whom she was to be in the next relationship. When she told me all this, I replied by saying, if she had the baby and it was mine, I would undoubtedly take care of my responsibility. She had him, but because of her relationship at the time, she did not really want me to be involved in her life, which meant I had limited involvement in the child's life.

At the time, I didn't really trip because I didn't know definitively the child was mine. Shortly after, during a period when she was on the outs in her personal relationship, I finally got a chance to meet my son for the first time. Immediately, I knew in my heart that the boy was mine. During that period, she was more amiable. It allowed me an opportunity to establish a connection with the child and begin to build a bond. The relationship was being developed through less than ideal circumstances for two reasons; her living conditions were unstable at the time, and I still was not completely certain I was the father of the child. I only had a deep feeling, which was enough for me to begin establishing a relationship and bond. As time passed, her personal relationship status changes had tremendous effects on her willingness to allow me to be a part of our child's life. If I ever became territorial believing myself due a certain level of accessibility to the child as a matter of parental right, she would quickly remind me that we weren't even certain he was mine. This effectively put up a reasonable argument in disallowing any claim I would, or could, make about my rights as a parent.

She did not make the early days pleasant. In her attempts to appease her boyfriend, she spent a lot of time being disagreeable to my attempts to be actively involved. Years later, I understand better what may have been going on in her head and heart. Wanting to be in a whole, happy family with her significant other without the uncertainty or jealousy that can be caused by a close connection with an ex was enough. Moreover, any personal anguish she may have felt about the way I treated her when we were an item were more than enough reason for her to be disagreeable and unaccommodating. Although I'm able to see clearly now what may have prompted the behavior, going through it at the time was unpleasant and extremely mentally and emotionally taxing.

Our relationship was a great learning experience for me. It tried my patience to the limit. It also caused me to grow up and see beyond the selfishness of my own feelings and desires. We live in an era of mixed family structures. Situations like teen pregnancy make the perfect circumstances and increase the likelihood that children will be raised in split and single parent homes. Each parent will usually go on to pursue other romantic interests and chances are that new families will be created with components like children from a past relationship. Other siblings from later unions lead to the development of a mixed family structure. Our relationship took on those dynamics very early on.

I credit Elsa with developing me into the man I am today, and we are still really good friends. Although our relationship was tumultuous most of the time, it was the singular experience that showed me how to be a man of long-suffering and selflessness. To ensure that my son would have the benefit of my presence in his life, I had to accept some very unfair terms. Before she and I had Eric, she had a daughter named Tierra from a previous relationship. After she had our son, she had another boy and girl in her next relationship after ours. She had three other children other than our son. Being the man I am, I was reared to treat all children the same. That meant when I was around my youngest son and his siblings, I couldn't treat any of them any different then I treated my own. A strong message that was consistent in my own family was that "we are the village." The fact that the other three were not mine biologically didn't matter. I was still responsible for loving them the same and doing for one the same as for all.

That didn't mean that I sent child support for all four children, but it did mean if I came with gifts for Eric, I came with gifts for the rest. If I came to pick up Eric for the weekend, I was willing to take the rest for the weekend, and what I told him in terms of the moral life lessons I shared, I told the rest the same.

Because of the dynamics of the modern family structure, we may tend to find ourselves challenged with dealing with a ready-made family. More times than not, the woman we meet has a child or children. If you choose a woman with a child, then it's a package deal. You essentially commit not only to the relationship with the woman but also to a relationship with the children too.

Whenever I became intimately involved with a woman with children, those children became my children too. The woman I married had two boys when we met. They, too, became a part of my family unit. I treated them with all the same love as my own boys and Eric's siblings. That is not a popular conversation amongst my peers—taking care of other people's children. Far too often, the common undertone among black men is that a woman's children are not their responsibility. In all honesty, they are not, unless you choose to be intimately involved with their mother. If so, then they become as much your responsibility as the biological father's. It's a moral commitment.

If you are not the man who is morally deficient and you have accepted the responsibility of being a father figure to children who are not biologically yours, it should not come at the expense of being an active father to your own. The act of being an involved father on any level is in addition to what you are obligated to do for your own. To be a biological father is obligatory. To add the responsibility of being a stepfather or surrogate father is a voluntary obligation that you commit to by virtue of your involvement in the lives of the mothers of the additional children.

Elsa was the first experience I had that helped shape the value and understanding I had for the mixed family structure. Our interaction showed me how to be accepting of adverse circumstances. It displayed very vividly that no matter what she and I had gone through, the children were innocent of any, and all offense. They would be the real victims of the dysfunction that she and I created if I didn't think past the petty differences that we had about our own relationship. I had to see the potential to cause great mental and emotional trauma down the line. It helped me realize that no matter how mad she made me,

I still needed to love her to some degree because not only did Eric love her, but the rest of her children did too. If I really loved them like I said I did, as a man, I was required to do whatever it took to be a part of their lives.

Fatherhood is a cradle to the grave commitment. It is a debt, duty, sacrifice, and reward like no other. As we grow together, we make a lot of mistakes that equate to sacrifices to the children that can lead to mental and emotional damage. I made so many mistakes throughout the process that it's not funny. I have learned something new from each one of them that has proven invaluable in the grand scheme of things. I often feel that these lessons came too little, too late in that the psychological and emotional damage caused by my inexperience and immaturity has already been done. Things my children will have to work through on their own in the future were inflicted at the hands of my ignorance. However injurious those experiences may have been, they will not have been in vain if I can make something out of their sacrifices.

Fatherhood is a continuous responsibility—hence this dialogue. I am still obligated to give them an exchange for value in terms of our parent-child relationship. The lessons within these pages are those that should have been established years ago and built upon over time. They always say it's "better late than never." Under these circumstances, I'm inclined to agree. I always say, "Unless you're dead, you always have a chance." This is my chance to communicate a message that distance has caused me to not be able to share.

The only priceless commodity we have in this brief physical form is TIME. I have caused us to lose a valuable portion of it. There is no way to get it back. Therefore, the next best thing is to create a timeless dedication of love that will continuously say just how important my boys are to me.

Time is measured in two different units when it comes to relationships; quantity and quality. Is one any more important than the other? Many may believe that quality time is the most important of the two, but, in reality, a healthy mix of the two is the best combination. Quantity may be hard to produce in this day and age. We live in a fast-paced society, which is becoming increasingly more competitive in terms of being able to survive. In an effort to make the necessary resources to sustain yourself and your children you may run short of time to devote to them. Let me encourage that you find every opportunity to spend quality and quantity time with them.

You'll get something like 6,570 days to spend with your child between birth and eighteen, their legal adulthood. I know all too well what it's like to forfeit a large block of that time. It is not a pleasant happening. I caused my boys to lose some of their most informative developmental years. To have to spend them without the physical presence, love, guidance, security and stability of their father's input.

Fatherhood is a one-shot deal. No matter how many times you are able to repeat the process, you only have one shot with each child to provide the elements and experiences necessary to help them become complete and fulfilled people. The time goes by too quickly. It seems like it takes forever for us to get to adulthood when we look at life through youthful eyes. But once we reach the other side, looking at our children grow up we realize just how fast it flies.

My children are among the most important things in my life. The saddest reality that I have had to face is that I couldn't see how important they were until I had already made a critical mistake. I have an affirmation that I use when things get hard in my life, "my blood, my life, my kids." It's what the Eye of the Tiger theme song is to the Rocky movie for me. It helps me remember what is important, what my purpose is and what I live for. It gives me the extra inspiration I need to make it that last few seconds in the twelfth round.

The element that has been the most condemning about this whole prison experience has not been doing time itself but leaving my boys out there to fend for themselves. That was the real punishment in having been sentenced to fifteen years in prison. My sons would have to look to other men to get the necessary tools to prepare to become successful men. That was a knife that cut very deep. A self-inflicted wound that continues to ail me even now. To the best of my knowledge, all my boys have had some good male influences in their lives.

I am grateful that there have been other men courageous enough to be positive influences on them. I have never wanted to be the man and father who did not take care of his responsibilities, especially in parenthood. Even so, I ended up being that very individual. Today, after much growth and development, I have reached a point where I can appreciate the value of another man who is willing to step in and be the caregiver to a little boy that is not his own. To those men I say, "God bless you." Your efforts may go unrecognized by many, but your sacrifices will be greatly rewarded. Now more than ever the world needs men who will do the extraordinary. You who are answering the call stepping up to the responsibility of extra duty are a rare breed.

Shentell was blessed to meet one such man. They were engaged after a brief courtship and have been happily married ever since. I did not have the pleasure of many personal encounters with the man she married. Altogether, I believe that Franky and I have spoken about five or six times at most; however, I have had numerous good updates and positive reports about his involvement in our son's life. Although I would have liked to be a lot more connected to their family unit in the process of my son's growing up, I cannot find one bad thing to say about Franky as a man, stepfather or father. He has provided his family a fairytale existence. I can only respect the way he raised my child as if he were his own. Even when he and his wife had more children, he continued to father his stepson the same as he always has. I owe him a great deal. I have a profound love, admiration, and respect for him. Thank God he is a villager too.

Fatherhood is a lifetime commitment. Our children will become adults and progress on to independence, but our commitment to fatherhood is never ending. I look at my own situation as an indication of just how real that commitment truly is. Here I am in my mid-thirties and still looking to my parents for mental, emotional, and even financial support.

RELATIONSHIPS

Every interaction between people constitutes some sort of relationship. Granted, we may not consider them to be, but human interaction consists of communicating with each other, which ultimately creates some kind of interpersonal relationship. These relationships have varying degrees of significance and intimacy, but they are all relationships, nonetheless. Thus far, we've explored very intimate relationships, those of the family, friendships, the marriage bond, and that of a father and his child. As we proceed to delve into the relationship arena, we'll broaden the scope to include those of a more general nature.

The way we interact with people outside of our intimate circle will determine the ease with which we are able to make things happen. There are numerous different types of general relationships: business, professional, community, public, positions of leadership, and so on. Each of these conditions lends itself to a certain type of relationship between you and others that has its own dynamic. We are challenged with the task of deciding how we would like to be recognized in each of these capacities, then creating relationships that are indicative of who we say we are. For example, if I am in a capacity of community leadership, I will need to foster good ties with others in leadership, my subordinates, and the community that we serve, and fortify those relationships over time in order to be effective and successful.

Relationships are a little recognized treasure that we tend to overlook. Sometimes we don't realize how important relationships truly are outside of those intimate ones that we readily recognize. If we are able to view all human interaction as relationships just as valuable as our intimate relationships, it would increase our quality of experience ten-fold. That is not to say that we should be as emotionally attached to our boss at work as we are to our child, wife or mother, but if we give our professional relationships the same consideration as we do our family, it would certainly improve the quality of the communication and interaction.

Quite naturally our intimate relationships are the ones that affect us the most. They are the ones that we are most closely emotionally attached to. They can hurt us the hardest and equally bring us the greatest amount of joy. It is for that reason we give those relationships so much consideration. As kids we do things to receive praise from our parents. Likewise, we refrain from certain things to avoid disappointing them. As adolescents, we do, or don't do, things in our peer relationships based on how others in our group will perceive it. As men, we will avoid behavior that will cause dissension in our romantic relationship so that we don't piss off our significant other, outright anyway. We give all these relationships due consideration because we care about the people, what they think and how they feel. If we apply that same level of due consideration to all our relationships, the quality of the exchange increases, thereby, increasing the value of the relationship as a whole.

Overall, it is our own character that determines how our relationships develop. I am often amazed at how some people are able to dismiss their own behavior to the actions of others in justification of their own unflattering behavior; in more general terms, when a person is acting or behaving inconsiderately in relation to the general public, how many times people justify their own actions through the actions of somebody else. If a stranger that shared my space in a line at a department store was being impatient, rude, and disrespectful, is that any reason for me to treat them the same or to change my own disposition from pleasant to hostile because they are doing so?

What does a stranger have to do with my attitude, character, and relationships? For a very brief minute while that stranger and I share personal space in line waiting to check out, there is an impersonal relationship that has been established between us. It is a social norm to which we give little attention, but it exists and is a very important part of our civilized social structure. It is our relationship that we share with the public and community. It goes back to the admonishment of your parents when they said, "You're a representation or reflection of me when you are out in public."

They said that to teach us that we are responsible to everyone for how we act at all times. The lesson of common courtesy is the foundation for appropriate behavior in our impersonal public relationships. It is inconsiderate and just plain bad taste to behave unpleasantly in public. Therefore, the majority of us rely on those early lessons on good manners out in public which make our impersonal relationships tolerable and, on many occasions, pleasurable.

How about the relationship of the President of the country and the people? None of us really knows the President on a personal or intimate level, although seeing him so much in the media we may feel like we do, yet many of us will show the President some amount of reverence and respect if we were ever to meet him face to face—those who don't despise him anyway. Likewise, we feel a certain level of entitlement to his attention to our needs and problems based on his title and duties. What makes this relationship different from any other relationship that we share in the public domain? After all, the President is but another stranger, except for his job.

It's the job. His relationship to all Americans is not just that of another person but is a position of responsibility and leadership. His decisions will affect all us in some way. Therefore, although he may be as strange to us as Joe the plumber from across town, we still share a relationship that is more defined by virtue of his title and our expectations of his duties to us. The President and the citizenry is just one example of a relationship that is impersonal, distant and public by nature but very significant in terms of how he and we view and consider each other.

Even among his worst critics, we would be hard pressed to find anyone who would throw a shoe at our President. If not out of respect, then surely out of fear of the consequences.

That is just a snapshot of a public relationship. Public relationships vary in makeup and significance, from the rude patron at the department store to those of people to whom we have more of an emotional attachment like pastors, teachers, neighbors and the such. These relationships are measured on a sliding scale that starts at unimportant and ends at those very important, family, friends, and romantic ones. The idea is to nurture all your relationships, so that they produce the maximum benefit for you and whoever is involved. It doesn't matter if it is a business, professional, academic, community, intimate or public relationship. Take measures to be attentive and considerate of the people involved and the relationship will reward you with the highest benefits possible.

There is no way for you to control the feelings or behavior of others. No matter how you feel about the people you are in relationships with, they may not always reciprocate the same loyalty that you do them. A stranger may not be courteous to you even though you are being kind to them. We are all different. We think differently, we value differently. Consequently, these differences tend to affect the nature of how we act towards, and with, each other. You can only control you. You are responsible for your actions. Concern yourself only with your actions in terms of your efforts to produce quality, working, and lasting relationships.

Always beware of the famed "frienemy." These people may be the most hazardous to your health of all. A "frienemy" is someone who poses as a friend but on the low is really an enemy. The danger in these relationships is that you can never tell their true intent in dealing with you. Like we discussed earlier in the section on friends, a true-blue friend is one-in-a-million. If you get a few in a whole lifetime, then you have been blessed beyond measure. Haters are a dimea-dozen. You'll get an abundance of "frienemies" throughout a lifetime. Just know that everyone who appears to be solid may not always have your best interest at heart. Feed those people with a long-handled spoon. When you allow a person into your intimate space, you become vulnerable. That is the time that you are exposed and susceptible to the greatest amount of hurt.

Bottom line, friend or foe, all these interactions constitute some kind of relationship. Their quality will determine how much pleasure you get from life, your success level, and the richness of your prosperity. By treating all relationships with due consideration, with reservation if it is determined that the other person does not have your best interest at heart, and overall attentiveness beyond self-interest, you put yourself in a better position for quality experiences for the long haul.

LEADERSHIP

Not everyone is called to serve through leadership. Leadership is a big responsibility that few will be chosen for. The scripture says, "Many are called, but few are chosen." When we look back over history, we are reminded of just how true this maxim is. Out of the billions of people to have walked this planet, the annals of history tell only a few stories of great men and women who have done magnificent things. That is enough of an indicator to say that not a lot of people will be great leaders of timeless or historic magnitude.

Even so, each of us is a leader in our own rite. As men, we are responsible for a great number of things. Taking care of ourselves, protecting our families (mom, wife, children etc.), role modeling and any number of other things that come with the territory of manhood. That being the case, even though we may not be a leader to many, we certainly are leaders to a few. It can start as early as childhood being a role model to a younger sibling. It can then extend through school with being a role model because of your athletic ability or your election as student body president. Leadership positions can be as small as being the idol of a younger neighborhood kid or as pronounced as sitting on the board of city council. Regardless of the connection, each of these relationships is just as important as those of great historic movements lead by immortal charismatic leaders.

If there is anyone following in your footsteps or dependent on you for direction, then ultimately leadership begins with you. It is the example you set by virtue of the character you exhibit. The greatest responsibility of leadership exists in your internal intimate unit. The people who are closest to you who see you on a regular basis are the ones most subject to your influence. You are responsible to them for providing a good example. It is your actions that will show the defining qualities they need to be positive, productive and progressive people.

There are a number of important character traits that encompass a good leader many of which we have already highlighted throughout the text of this book. In addition to those characteristics, here are a few more that any good leader should have, in no particular order of importance:

Humility	Foresight	Tenacity
Ability to listen	Fortitude	Integrity
Selflessness	Compassion	Receptiveness
Organizational Skills	Inspirational Abilities	Visionary

Although leadership begins with you, it extends beyond you to the people who you lead. Not only are you responsible for your own actions, but as a leader you become responsible for the actions of those you serve as well.

For those of us who decide to go beyond our intimate circle and render our services in leadership to a greater number of people, that responsibility increases tremendously. The more we grow and find ourselves ready, able and willing to take on the challenges that come with leadership in a greater capacity, the more responsibility we will have. At the same time, the more reward we will feel as a result of our contribution and commitment to service.

Overall, leaders are servants. They are supposed to serve the people they represent. If it is a father/child, the father serves as protector/provider. If it is a teacher/student, the teacher serves as an educator; in a pastor/congregation, the pastor serves as a spiritual guide. Even our political leaders serve as our representatives in domestic and international political affairs. True leaders are always servants, not the other way around.

With leadership comes power. We should be careful not to forget that too much power has the tendency to corrupt. If we keep the tenet of servitude in the forefront of our mind, it will help us to stay grounded when the trappings of power begin to sidetrack or distort our views or agendas. This is the time when the traits of humility and selflessness will come to your aid. Keeping the mind of a servant will help bring back into perspective the true nature of a leader's duties.

Another critical element in the composition of a great leader is his willingness to be led. All great leaders have someone that they learn from. It is a paradox that is as timeless as time itself. In order to be an effective and successful leader you must learn the skills needed from someone who is wiser and more seasoned than you. It is a growth process that entails identifying the end goal. Every great leader has a great mentor. Submit to wise counsel and you will have half of what it takes to be an effective leader.

Besides a willingness to submit to a wiser, more experienced guiding force, true leaders must always lead by example. The world is very critical of people. It is not enough to preach a good game. You must model what it is you say you stand for. Leadership is a show, not tell function. Bear in mind that people are fallible and subject to make mistakes. The hallmark of a great leader is shown not by trying to avoid falling short but taking immediate responsibility when you do and pledging to correct the shortcoming. People are cruel, but eventually forgiving. Those who act in humility are forgiven much more quickly than those who evade responsibility for their mistakes.

I am constantly reminded that people are watching me at all times, that I am a representation in my actions of what I value the most. I find it hard to live in hypocrisy. Therefore, when I profess something as a value, I am held to a self-imposed standard of expectation that my actions should show that which I say. As I have come to a place of awareness of the power and significance of those things I understand better, how critical my words and actions are in relation to my leadership responsibilities. I hope to live the rest of my life setting examples that are healthy, positive, balanced and complete. When it's all said and done, I want to have added more to this world than I have taken away.

EDUCATION

What is the importance of education? Although we have attached all kinds of price tags to education in this country, the value of education is priceless. We have grown accustomed to the high costs associated with a good education from private school in the primary years, all the way to the ivy league six figure universities. We rarely give it much thought that even though there is a monetary value associated with getting a good education, a tragedy takes place when some of us are priced out of the privilege.

I have not always been a fan of formal and traditional education. As a youth I could not clearly see the value of education. This didn't really change much until sometime in my early thirties. I'd say I was a bit slow in that department, but, looking back on it, I have to concede to being just plain stupid. Growing up under the oppressive tutelage of a stern academic for a father, I was turned off by the education institution very early on. My father was an education Nazi and his insistence on pushing me the extra mile to help encourage future success did just the opposite for me.

In my pre-teens I began to become rebellious. The rebellion eventually led to a distinct disdain for authority, organization, and order, all which were the foundation of the education institution. I eventually let my rebellion and laziness get the best of me and school was one of the first things I pushed out of my life.

In some ways it was my way of taking control of my life. My grandmother still reminds me years later when I said as a kid, "Grandma, when I turn sixteen, I'm droppin' out of school and moving to Paris and becoming a bum." My father spent five years living in Paris, hence my fascination with it. When it was all said and done, I kept my word, minus moving to Paris, I did drop out of school and was not living much better than a bum.

Education and I have had a tumultuous history. It has been a rocky road that I'll spare the details of. I'll just say that education and I had to grow on one another. As an adult I can appreciate all those extra hours my father made me do extra homework; all the culturally diverse experiences he exposed me to, immersion in the arts, theater, opera, symphonies, museums, art exhibits, travel experiences, formal dining, rare literature and the numerous things I used to dread while growing up as everybody else's parents were taking them to the movies and sporting events. As a youngster, I felt robbed. As an adult, I feel much more well-rounded.

I didn't see those experiences as being part of my education. Only now does it make sense that education is more than the grade level you complete in school. As intelligent as I have the potential to be, I still missed the formal education boat for far too long. I dropped out of school in about the ninth, tenth or eleventh grade. Reason being, every year after the ninth grade, school officials always tried to figure out ways to merge my course load in order to help me graduate with my class. God bless those people. It was never going to happen. I could not take the environmental structure of traditional school.

I enrolled in Job Corps when I turned eighteen and went from my home in Charlotte, North Carolina to Miami, Florida. I spent three months in Job Corps working toward taking the G.E.D. exam. I did not take a trade, just went to G.E.D. class every week. I went to Job Corps to get a fresh start and get out of the environment that was adding to my distractions. The only thing that I didn't change was my mentality or behavior. Needless to say, I didn't last long.

They had a Zero Tolerance policy for misbehavior, and I eventually got kicked out for failing a urinalysis. The worst part is that I got kicked out the week before I was scheduled to take the G.E.D. test. That stunt brought me a one-way ticket back to Charlotte without a G.E.D. and no marketable skills. The one thing I will credit myself with as a halfway intelligent decision is that as soon as I got back to Charlotte, I went to the local community college and applied to take the exam. I slam dunked the pre-test and took the real exam over the following two weeks. As the story goes, I passed the test, all thanks to the three months I spent in Job Corps in Reverend Rackly's G.E.D. prep class. I know if I hadn't gone to Job Corps, I would not have been able to pass the test. I took the pre-test twice before I left to Job Corps and failed miserably. I needed the time and space to focus.

At that point, my academic career was done. I had enough to get me into the labor market, and I figured I could do manual labor for the rest of my life. So much for high aspiration and ambition. Then tragedy struck. I finished my G.E.D. in August of 1995 and was working at Roadway Packaging Systems loading and unloading trucks. On October 8, 1995, I was shot four times in the back, and two bullets hit my spinal cord. I was paralyzed instantly. And there went my future plan to do manual labor for the rest of my life. I didn't stay in the hospital for long. One month and one week and I was at home, readjusting to life in my new condition.

While I readjusted, I had to consider what was going to happen next. I was just about to turn nineteen, and I still had a lot of life in me. I moved quickly to re-establish my independence. Then in the spring of '96,' I enrolled in Central

Piedmont Community College. Now that I could no longer depend on my physical ability, I had to acquire other marketable skills.

School was short lived. As I said before, life and my children caused me to take a detour and hold off on my education. It was probably for the best though. I was not interested in school for getting educated. I was in school to get a degree to look good on a resume. In hindsight, this would have been a waste of time and money. I was back and forth to community college from '96' to '03,' never really making any substantial headway at completing any program. Honestly, my first reason for going to school was to keep free flying benefits while my mother was working for the airline industry. I thought that one day I'd finish a degree in something and look more attractive to a potential future employer. I didn't know I was only kidding myself. I don't have an employee's attitude, which meant any job I had I'd have to create for myself. The very last time I went to school was to look more worthy of leniency at my sentencing in 2004. Until that point, those were the only things education seemed to offer me.

When I self-surrendered to FCI Butner-Low, I was pleased to see that the prison offered courses and two complete degree programs. The local community college Vance-Granville Community College came to the prison, and the State of North Carolina was footing the bill with Pell Grant money. I was all set. I had thirteen years to do it, and getting an Associate of Arts degree seemed like a perfect way to do them. I went to the education department on registration day and asked to be enrolled in the Liberal Arts two-year transfer degree program and was told that they no longer offered it. The prison was already cutting back on program availability, which increased the sense of urgency in my mind. Then another shocking blow—I was told that class size was very limited and priority was given to those with outdates closer to release.

It seemed hopeless. The only program still offered was a two-year Associates of Applied Science Degree in Business Administration. My outdate was so far off, I couldn't imagine I'd get a seat in one of the twenty or so available seats jockeying against the 1,300 plus other inmates in the prison. I signed up to take the placement test anyway. Math was my worst subject and to complete the degree, I would have to take something like nine math-related classes. I figured it would be practically impossible to get into classes anyway, so I took the test.

The results were posted and registration took place shortly after. Just as I had expected, I did poorly on the math portion, making remedial math a prerequisite, upping my math load to ten classes. However, I had one more hurdle to cross, getting into the classes. The college officials held an open registration and we were all given the opportunity to sign up for the classes we wanted. They would then go through the names looking at our outdates. The ones with the closest outdates would get the classes. The rest of us would have to wait. The list was posted, and to my complete disbelief, I was enrolled in three classes. I was on my way.

For the next two and a half years, I would repeat the nervous wait at registration time. By the grace of God, each new semester I would get all the classes I registered for. I often wondered why more people didn't take advantage of the free education, but I never advocated for it to those who didn't. It was their lack of participation that allowed me to have a seat. I did not realize how important seizing the moment was until a few years later. I finished the program, earning an associate degree in December of 2007, courtesy of the Federal Bureau of Prisons and the State of North Carolina. This was a five to six-thousand-dollar investment that I could not have paid for.

After I completed my Associates degree, I considered going on to try for a Bachelor's. The only difference was that the prison did not have a four-year program. If I was to continue, it would have to be at my own expense. I checked into a couple of correspondence programs at several universities. What I found was way beyond my ability to pay. Considering we were in the thick of a financial recession, it was a bad time to reach out to my support network, my parents, and ask for assistance—especially since they were already supporting me and my children, so I took some time off to learn Spanish and work on writing several books.

I spent a great deal of time reading books on writing, the publishing industry and studying other writers' styles. I approached the Spanish language with one hundred percent of my effort. I took a Hispanic cellmate, watched music video, kids' programs on the weekends, and novellas (soap operas) during the week. I listened to music, read conversation books and did workbooks. I took every opportunity to engage the Latino community as much as I could. This was my way of continuing to invest in my education and make good use of my time with the little that I had at my disposal.

Before I left the Federal Prison Complex in Butner North Carolina, the whole college program was discontinued. Butner was one of the last remaining institutions in the whole Bureau of Prisons that still offered a college degree with state funds. In 2010, the college program was completely defunct. This unfortunate end to a much-needed service came in spite of the fact that the more education, trade training or skills ex-offenders receive, the greater the likelihood that they will not re-offend. Governor Bev Perdue made it one of her last term agendas to defund Pell Grant spending on incarcerated students.

115

At that moment, I was all too glad that I didn't waste time getting mine. Although state spending on educating the incarcerated was a mere fraction of the overall budget allocations, the Governor's office felt it deserved the axe. I can't say that I blame them. Their reason was that statistically the program was a failure. Just based on what I saw at my own institution, which is the only Federal Complex in the State, people did abuse the privilege. If thirty students were accepted into a class session, only twelve to fifteen completed. The graduation rate was even lower. Because students were routinely being transferred to other institutions or released, it increased the chances that they would not finish the complete degree program. If I had to guess the percentage of successful graduates of the college program, I'd say that thirty-five percent would have been stretching it.

If you look at the statistics, you would have every right to believe that the program was a failure. Each student that registered for classes took one individual allotment of funds. When those people later dropped the classes, that money is considered wasted. When you look at how many times that happened versus how many people completed, anyone in their right mind would be justified in concluding that there was a better use for the funds, like giving it to a disadvantaged young person who hasn't done anything to breach the public's trust. At the end of the day, I hold us responsible for the loss of the Pell Grant funding. Education is undoubtedly an integral part of helping people become successful and productive contributing members of society. But, if we weren't willing to utilize the program to show state officials that it was money well spent, we deserved to lose it.

The recession eventually let up, and I got an opportunity to enroll in a college correspondence program. At my parents' expense, I was able to see just how costly school can be. Thanks to the Associates degree from Vance-Granville, I was able to enroll in Ohio University's College Program for the Incarcerated (CPI). I took courses towards my Bachelor's whenever the finances permitted. It wasn't cheap. OU took the full body of my previous credits since I had earned a degree but still required that I complete a major body of core curriculum at their institution. At about $2,100 every two courses I was looking at over $15,000 to complete my undergrad studies.

Never before had school seemed to occupy such a place of importance in my mind. As I reached a point where I could no longer proceed in my studies for a lack of financial resources, I had a very important decision to make. How do I keep educating myself without financial means? The answer was easy; as simple as the opera, a Broadway play or a trip to a foreign country. My father once said when we were vacationing in Barbados and he asked what I wanted to eat, and I said "McDonalds," he responded, "When you travel, you should experience new things. It's the only way to learn what's out there in the world. The world is more than just McDonalds."

Education and learning happen on more than just a school level. It was that mentality that helped me figure out what to do next. Learning is an everyday process. If we are willing to be taught, we can find many opportunities to increase our knowledge base. I have taken time to complete a paralegal self-study course, write a few more books, read all kinds of investing and financial literacy literature and start learning Chinese among other things. Bearing in mind that the world is a cornucopia of education opportunities, one can find more than enough learning opportunities, even in prison.

The internet is another useful tool for education. There is no excuse for the person that has the world at their fingertips to lack education. Resources like Wikipedia, Khan Academy, MOOC's (Massive Open Online Courses), the public library, community development/enrichment programs and a host of others exist for anyone to use in order to advance to the next level. If you're uneducated in this day and age, it's because you want to be, not because you have to be. Education helps you acquire the tools to increase your marketability. You look more attractive to prospective employers. Building your knowledge base will make you more confident and more capable. That confidence will drive success.

Beyond traditional and self-education, the very best teacher of all is experience. There is nothing like firsthand knowledge. In fact, the more you repeat anything, the better at it you become. They say that if you devote ten thousand hours to any one craft, you will become an expert. In order to be good at something, you practice. In order to be great at something, you devote yourself. Firsthand knowledge is the very best, but a very close second is observation. It's not always necessary to touch the fire to know it's hot. If you just watched your partner get burned by touching the fire, then it would do you good to learn from their mistake. The wisest among us will learn from both firsthand experiences and the experiences of others.

I think for me one of the greatest revelations of my time was when I concluded that education was, and is, a lifelong process, finally, miles away from the kid holding a G.E.D. in his hand vowing never to step foot into an institution of higher learning again. The minute we stop learning, we commit mental suicide. We stagnate ourselves and essentially become stuck in a time warp and relegate ourselves to mental infancy wherein no maturation can take place. When we recognize that education is a lifelong process, we can graduate to the next life cycle: teaching.

The requirement of those of us who are willing to continue to learn is that we teach others what we know. If we do not make ourselves capable by preparing ourselves through perpetual education, then we are ill-fitted to teach and lead the next generation. Unless we have the knowledge, we will be teaching those who follow us unhealthy and destructive things. If you know better, then you can do better. Like the Bible saying goes, "My people perish for lack of knowledge."

HARD WORK

There is no substitute for hard work. My mother often tells me to work smarter not harder. This is advice that I take to heart considering I'm no longer able to do manual labor. My dad used to tell me that "thinking is hard work." After many years doing more thinking than anything else, I'm inclined to agree with his counsel. The reality of this seeming oxymoron is that working smarter is just as hard work as exerting large amounts of physical energy in manual labor.

The human body can only take so much activity before it will begin to slow down, eventually demanding that you rest before doing any more. The brain is much the same in that it is a part of the body that needs rest in order to function at optimal capacity. However, the thing that separates the brain from the rest of the bodily functions is that it retains what it gets from its use. The results you get from work that your physical activities can produce has to be constantly repeated in order to produce, whereas the results you achieve from the work you do with your brain stay with you forever. They can also continue to produce for you without putting any more physical or mental work into the activity in some cases.

For example, the person who works in construction building houses has to work continually in order to build homes. If he stops working, then the next house won't be built. The harder he works, the faster he can complete projects. The more he can do, the more he can earn. While in the alternative, the person who authors a book will put some mental energy into writing a good manuscript, a little physical energy into creating a decent product and a little more energy into bringing the product to the reader. Then, as the book sells, he benefits repeatedly from sales without doing much more work. I use the second example lightly. Believe me; writing, publishing, and selling a book is hard work, but it is a type of hard work that has the potential for abundant reward beyond anything physical labor alone can offer.

I don't suggest that everybody stop what they currently do and pursue a writing career. That probably wouldn't be a very good look. Besides the fact that if you're going to write you need to have something to say, writing takes a little bit of skill that not everybody has. How about another example to which we can all relate? Most of us are familiar with billionaire Warren Buffett, the CEO of Berkshire Hathaway. Mr. Buffett is one of the foremost authorities on investing. He has been nicknamed the Oracle of Omaha for his famed ability to pick the right companies to invest in. I'm not sure of his background, but I believe it's fair to say that he spends a great deal of time studying companies, market conditions, and any other relevant information that he needs to make an informed decision about his investment prospects.

Any one of us can take a little bit of time and research something that interests us that has the potential to improve our economic condition. I doubt we'll become the next Warren Buffett if we decide to take an interest in playing the stock market, investment real estate, the used car business, or any other industry that we may invest in. However, with a little hard work, I'm sure we can become knowledgeable enough to make some good choices that will pay residual dividends beyond the work we invest in the time it took to learn how to make it happen. The point is to work a little harder for a short while by acquiring the information necessary so that you don't always have to work so hard. That's really working smarter.

Nothing worthwhile comes to you without some level of sacrifice. It's easy to look at the mega successful people of the world and see the finished product. Rarely are we privy to the process of what they went through to get there. What separates the normal from the exceptional a lot of times is not intelligence, opportunity or resources but sheer determination and a willingness to try. What do you think when you hear names like Bill Gates, Warren Buffett, Jay-Z," Beyoncé, Barack Obama, and Oprah Winfrey? They are successful, wealthy or influential, to say the least. I see those people like that and more, but what I see more than that when I think of these people is that these are the type of people who don't stop short of working a little harder to perfect their craft.

The difference between the exceptional and the rest is that they don't stop, they don't compromise on their goals and they are willing to sacrifice it all to arrive at the place they are trying to get to. The process is often a painful one. Steve Jobs was the founder of one of the world's most influential computer electronics companies—Apple. He was also later thrown out of the same company he helped create, only to be brought back to take the company to new heights until the very last day of his life. He didn't abandon his dream when things got out of whack. He kept his focus and kept on headed toward his final destination even in the face of adverse circumstances. That's what hard work buys you.

The tradeoff for hard work is that it cannot return void. If you work hard at something, your return-on-investment (ROI) is guaranteed. You may not see the payoff immediately, but the dividends are inevitable. There is no way to invest positive input in yourself and not accumulate the necessary things you need to be successful. In fact, hard work is a prerequisite for success. Be it mental or physical energy, no benefits can come to the individual who has not put in his fair share of hard work first. Nothing from nothing leaves nothing.

120

Hard work is irreplaceable. Half-ass won't get it. You get back out of anything what you put into it. The more you bet, the greater the odds are of loss, but equally so, the bigger the payout is when you win. Sometimes that entails putting in a lot of grunt work and sweat equity before you see the payout. For me, I always refer to when I started learning Spanish to when I'd get frustrated about where I was with other things in my life. When I first started to learn, I would get frustrated and want to give up. Every time I did, I would take a step back, relax, then try again. Eventually I got better, until the point where I could communicate. I applied the same dedication to writing a book. More than seven years later and a whole lot of disappointments down the line, I finally published a book and have built a modest name as a freelance writer. I have not reached the point of satisfaction yet, but I'm just at the beginning.

The beginning is about paying your dues. For me, the beginning was longer than I cared to endure—thirteen years in the making to be exact. The small successes from prison, like publishing a few magazine articles and building relationships with community organizations as a prison reform advocate, were minor compared to what I could have done with freedom on my side.

Dedicated hard work is the insurance plan that insures you will live up to your fullest potential. If you dedicate a small amount of energy doing what other people won't do, you will be miles in front of everybody else. The results of hard work is the payoff you owe yourself.

The catch is that nobody can create that ROI but you. Remember, anything worth having requires sacrifice. Results take time to measure. The instant gratification or entitlement mentality will not produce results that are lasting or of any substantial value. Long-term payoff should always be the focus. Creating a lasting legacy is more valuable than enjoying a temporary stint of good luck. Besides, luck is when preparation meets opportunity.

So, in reality, there is no such thing as good luck. You may come across some things and opportunities that make immediate come ups appear to be hard earned successes, but the amount of work rendered is always the best measuring stick. If any amount of hard work was applied, you will appreciate the end result more, and they are bound to have more of a lasting effect.

FAITH & SPIRITUALITY

Faith and spirituality should mean to you what you make of them. The world is full of clutter with regards to religious doctrine, which is what forms that basis of our knowledge and belief concerning things of the higher order. The principles that encompass the spiritual realm are not tangible, which makes them all the more challenging to understand. There are a few things that are good practices in terms of developing your spirit life. In my opinion, they are practices that have helped me along to great success. However, spiritual development is a delicate process that I'd advise anyone to decide on their own.

Developing your spiritual life is a personal experience. Many times we follow the examples that are set for us by our parents and family as first teachers. The religious dogma that is established in our family is usually our first line of input in terms of developing the basis of our spiritual belief system. If you are raised in a Christian, Muslim, Jewish or other type of belief system you are probably firmly grounded in that particular belief. There is nothing wrong with believing in something that is going to help you be or become a better person. That is supposed to be the reason or objective behind most organized religions. I won't comment on the tenets and beliefs of any religious belief. I've made it a practice not to offend an individual's sense of reason, and confronting religious beliefs and the differences many of them avow, if not done delicately, can definitely do that.

One thing I will say of the religious establishment is that they all contain an element of truth that is universal. I have explored the teachings of the Christians, Muslims, Jews, Buddhists, 5%er's, the Rastafarian movement, the Kabala, Secret Sciences, and Sufism, among others. I read the Bible, Qur'an, Torah, Hermetic Philosophy, writings of Manly P. Hall, Neville Goddard, and many others in my quest for spiritual enlightenment. Throughout my studies, I have come to recognize that there is an underlying message that is consistent no matter how different the spin is, given the delivery style of the source.

There is a method I use to determine truth that is a pretty simple formula to remember. There are three sides to any story. The one skewed to the left, the one skewed to the right and the theme that stays consistent—the middle ground. Take a car accident with two witnesses who saw it happen. Ask one person what happened, and they will tell you based on their perception of what they believe they saw. Ask the other, and you may get a similar story with slight variations based on their perception of what they believe they saw. The thing you hear consistently from both sides is the middle ground that is most likely the singular truth about what happened.

That is the approach I have taken with my spiritual growth and development. I have explored the numerous religious authorities insofar as the message and principles are concerned. I have looked for the consistency, absent all the dogmatic extras, and I have held on to the principles that appear to be universal truths across the board in all the different teachings. I know some believe that kind of approach is sacrilegious. I think of it as being well-rounded and educated on as many possibilities as you can. In this country there is an indeterminate number of religious movements, recognized and unrecognized. There is no way to engage them all. Besides, using the middle ground system to identify truth, it's not necessary to explore them all before you get the picture.

I grew up in a traditional Christian Holiness household. My mother, grandmother, great grandmother and everyone else that I knew were all Pentecostals. I was in the church from as far back as I could remember until I became rebellious as a teen and began to defy the mandate to attend. Church was the second thing behind school to get the boot when I was so-called taking control of my life as a juvenile (or as a delinquent was more like it). In my teen years, around fifteen, if my memory serves me correctly, I was discontented with the church experience and I felt a bitter emptiness in my spirit. I believed in the reality of the spirit realm, submitting to the idea that there were forces in existence that were greater than myself, but still deep down inside, there was a void that was not being filled with the measures of input I was getting spiritually at the time.

That emptiness took me on a journey to find something fulfilling that would help me balance out the physical with the spiritual in order to live a balanced and complete life. Save the details of my spiritual development process, I explored a number of things on the quest. Using the middle ground approach, I began to follow the recurring theme to what to me amounted to a universal truth. At this point in my life, I am open to any information that is spiritually enlightening. I am careful not to dwell too long on unhealthy elements. If the teachings are consistent with universal truth and can make me a better man by the application, I am willing to adopt it. If it violates the middle ground truth, I will reject it and feel good doing so.

Each man should decide for himself what he chooses to submit to in his spiritual life. He should not be relegated to a certain belief system simply because everyone in his family before him was Catholic or Hindu. His medium of spiritual enlightenment and development should be his choice. If you refuse to explore what exists out there along the lines of spiritual education, how will you be able to discriminate and differentiate between truth for you, and truth for someone else. Failure to look beyond what is right in front of us will lead us to a space of limited understanding. We will be no larger than the space and body of information that we occupy. The only way to enlarge our territory of understanding is to go beyond the closest and most comfortable thing to us.

I often refer to scriptures when I think about parables and timeless maxims that have been guiding forces in my life. Although I left the denomination of the establishment long ago, I still refer to the maxims for reminders, like "seek and ye shall find." All one has to do is be diligent in their desire to grow in their spirit life and look for the things that will make that growth possible. Your ability to do that will help you in the long run maintain an attitude of willingness to define your own spirituality for yourself.

If you keep in mind that spirituality is a lifetime journey, keep earnestly pursuing spiritual development, then you should have the necessary elements to create stability in uncertain times. Spiritual strength increases your mental capability. In order to fight uncertainty, you must be mentally fit and equipped to face the challenges that lie ahead. Doing this kind of spiritual exercise will help you establish, develop, and maintain your faith.

The simple definition of faith is the ability to believe. In less religious terms, faith is just a strong belief. High levels of faith increase your internal strength and can help you overcome the most trying challenges that life may throw at you. Faith is a sustenance that gives us a level of freedom that is unrivalled. Faith is the enemy of uncertainty and doubt. It is the audacity to believe that you can overcome whatever you're faced with. There is no compromise to faith, either you have it or you don't—but no middle ground. And the secret of faith and how it works is that you must have your own in order for it to work for you. No one can believe in you. It is up to you to believe in yourself before faith can be of any use to you.

CONTRIBUTION

Ultimately, all that we do, or have done leads to this point; contribution. The process of cultivating the person you are, attending to all the areas of your character discussed herein is ultimately to aid you in accomplishing your contribution. Your contribution will be your legacy. When the last chapter is written, it will be all that you've done that will best tell who you were. You have to decide what that story will be.

Your contribution gives you a purpose. It is the reason why you are. It has taken me longer than I would have liked to figure out what my contribution would be. I've always longed to do great things like the historic greats that we learn about all our lives. Those like my great grandfather Raymond E. Dandridge Sr., who played Negro League baseball and was inducted into the Baseball Hall Fame in 1987 or others like Malcolm, Martin and President Obama. These men have all inspired me by their own journeys to greatness. I hope to be blessed with enough time left in my life to attempt to achieve a tenth of any one of their levels of greatness.

What I have found in studying all the greatest legacies of men like these is that it was the combination of character building, willingness to accept the challenges they were called to and numerous little steps that led them to the places that have caused their names to be forever immortalized. The revelation for me was that you can never achieve an immortal legacy without taking the first step.

I understand now that any amount of contribution, great or small, begins with modest efforts that are increased over time. It wasn't until that became clear to me that I began to feel like what I am contributing makes any difference at all. After I matured a little, I began to want to add more to the things I had influence on than I was taking away. I believe Maslow's *Hierarchy of Needs* describes the condition as self-actualization, the point when you have met all your other needs and are at the place when you need to fulfill a need greater than your own. I decided that what I want to give back to others is a model of motivation that has the power to inspire a person never to give up. To me, that meant being vocal and active with people who have personal issues that may seem insurmountable.

It has taken me a very long time to figure out that the best way to show someone something was simply to do it myself, even though it was told to me a million times as a kid by everybody from parents to teachers. It's the old phrase "you lead by example." The thing that kept me from really setting out to pursue this purpose much earlier is the fact that molding myself into the kind of person someone should listen to and follow was going to be hard work.

It would require me to do the things that most others in my condition were not. To spend countless hours immersed in the search of knowledge so that I would be wise enough to give someone intelligent and prudent counsel, to push the extra mile so that the individual that refuses to try can think, "Hey look at him. If he can do it, then I know I can." That was not a comfortable process. It was so much easier to avoid the responsibility of hard work and haphazardly go through life settling for whatever happened to come my way.

The journey through prison was a dead end that helped open my eyes to embrace the desire to take more from life. I had wasted so much time and potential that a sense of urgency began to consume me, and I could no longer be content with myself without living up to my fullest potential. It was like the saying I wrote in 'Chablis: The Significance of You'; "People only change when the pain of staying the same becomes greater than the pain of change itself." Even though I had spent the majority of my incarceration being productive and achieving minor successes, there came a point when I had to make a choice; continue to waste my talents and let life just pass me by or get it together and at least make an honorable legacy that my family and I could be proud of. I'll never forget the day I watched the C.O. throwing my personal property through the tray trap in the Administrative Segregation Unit of the prison. I was in the hole for an infraction in prison, yet again, picking up the pieces of my life. That day, the pain of who I was became more than I could bear, and the process of change began to accelerate.

I woke up that day. I stopped dreaming and started planning. I want to have created a meaningful legacy by the time the last chapter of my life is written. At this point, I am willing to put in the work no matter how difficult that may be. I'm ready for the challenge. What has helped me to continue in times when it seems like there is no foreseeable reward in sight is the satisfaction of seeing any little victory or accomplishment. I had to come to the realization that every contribution won't lead to the next Civil Rights Movement, but everyone is just as important. To help a person work through a personal problem, to teach someone something they didn't know or simply being kind to a person who is not being kind to you are all forms of meaningful contributions that anyone can make. I hope someday to reach a level of capability where I can make greater, more wide spread contributions, but for now, I'll settle for continuing to try to make a difference one person at a time.

Your lifetime is limited, but your legacy is unending. It is up to us individually to determine how long our legacy will last. If it will be a good one or one that people would much rather forget shortly after you're gone. The best contributions are those done of selflessness, charitably and in fairness. If you pride yourself on operating is those ways, your contribution will undoubtedly produce positive and prosperous results. Selflessness is not always easy to exhibit. It requires a sacrifice on your part that is not necessarily a natural behavior in humans. It's easy to be selfless when it comes to the people we love and care about, but it's not as easy to be that way with everyone. I won't begin to suggest that anyone will be able to be completely selfless in all their doings, but as many times as is practicable is the goal we should all be aiming for.

Charity is the part of your contribution that you do without concern for what you can gain out of it. Giving for no other reason than a desire to be of some good and benefit to another. Even in charitable contributions, we are not exempt from compensation. Every time we give to a person or a cause out of the goodness of our heart, we get the satisfaction of knowing that we have done something good to improve the life of somebody else. To a certain extent, charity can often be one of the most rewarding types of contributions one can make.

In deciding your contribution, whether charitable or otherwise, don't forget to include the element of fairness. There is nothing more noble than to be a person who is capable of making his decisions with the consideration of what is fair and just for everyone who is involved. It is a quality that will serve you well if ever you find yourself in a position of authority or leadership. Remember that you get back what you put out. If you manage to be fair in your doings, the likelihood is that you will receive the same treatment in kind. Keep in mind that this may not always be the case, but in the times when you are not treated with fairness, remember that you are only responsible for your actions in any situation.

At the end of the day, it is each of our individual contributions that makes the world go around. No one can do your part but you. If you really want to capitalize on the real value of life, you will do well to make an earnest effort to contribute the best of what you have to offer. I promise the return on investment will be more than you ever bargained for.

CHANGE

The most certain thing in life is change. Even if it is an unwelcome occurrence, it is the only thing in life that is promised. People are creatures of habit. We create behavior patterns that are comfortable and familiar and seldom do we want to change. It is a paradox we must deal with if we are ever to live comfortably, balanced and complete. Seasons will change, things will live, things will die. Change is an inescapable phenomenon that we should embrace.

Regardless of the imminence and certainty of change, we still seem to resist it tooth and nail. This is undoubtedly because of the discomfort that accompanies the uncertainty of trying something new. Like I said in the previous section, change only happens when the pain of staying the same becomes greater than the pain of change itself. The thing about change is that if you're not willing to change on your own, then life will create situations that will force you to change. Oftentimes, those situations will entail some painful experiences. Then the process of change itself may be painful, too, because you are being forced into unfamiliar territory.

The caveat here is to be aware that growth is often a painful process either way. A willingness to relinquish the past for better things in the future may not always be the easiest thing to have to do, but, on many occasions, it is the best.

Speaking from experience, my life is a prime example of what happens to those of us who resist change. Not only are you pushed further behind the eight ball, but in my case, you cause headache, heartache, and dysfunction to the very people you say you love. In hindsight, I look back and say, "If I was only smart enough to embrace a new direction earlier." However, youth knows no folly, and ignorance is bliss.

There is no substitute for wisdom, which is most often gained at the expense of numerous learning experiences. Wisdom is a hard-earned treasure that's more valuable than silver and gold. In my eyes, knowledge and wisdom are the only true riches in the world. With each of them, we are able to accumulate all the material wealth, status, fame, and all else that we consider valuable. Having the wisdom to know when to change, what to change, and how to change will make the process so much more pleasant and tolerable. Wisdom and change are companions that complement each other when exercised in tandem. The moment I was wise enough to embrace change in my life, I was able to accomplish so much more, even with the disadvantage of a long prison sentence in the most productive years of my life. Incarceration created a crippling distance between me and my ability to produce, but it did not completely disable me from making wise investments into myself.

I just needed to be willing to shift my thinking about what was possible, even in prison. A willingness to change from traditional thinking to thinking outside of the box helped me accomplish some things that I may not have done otherwise. Change is an evolutionary process. It will not happen all at once. It takes deliberate, decisive action. There is no one-size-fits-all measure of change that ensures that what works for me will work for you. It's up to you to decide the areas in your life that need to be changed, then take the proper steps to make it happen.

A lot of times, change consists of confronting old behavior habits that are not healthy or indicative of highly successful living. I still have challenges I am working on to this day that I have not been able to conquer all the way. For instance, misogynistic conversations with my peers. Even though I don't feel like it is correct to degrade women, I still haven't been courageous enough to speak up when the fellows are engaged in denigrating conversations. I still struggle with intimacy and monogamous relationships. I have not totally conquered the adolescent tendency to objectify women. I am constantly challenged by criminal thinking habits and am bridled with a deep mistrust for law enforcement officials. I have little faith in the political process, and even though we have elected our first black President, I still believe there are glass ceilings for black men in this country, especially for those with felony convictions.

Be that as it may, I have to continually remind myself that no matter how many of these things may be true, I'm only responsible for me. The only limitations that exist are the ones we fix in our minds. The process of change for me has been an ever-present awareness that these elements and bad habits still exist. I have to make an effort every day to go in the opposite direction of the negative things that burden me regularly.

I've been making progress. I realize that it is a process, and I am a work in progress. I hope that as I go about taking small steps in the right direction, the process will get easier, and I'll eventually be completely content with the man I become. Until I can demand in every conversation with the fellows that they respect women, believe in the political system and restore faith and trust in the laws and officials that uphold them, I know I have major work to do.

I believe I'm on the right track. I have at least resolved that I won't exhibit misogynistic behavior. I will defer to the court system when I have a legal issue.

I'll be compliant and cooperative with law enforcement officials even if I am being treated with disdain and contempt. I won't commit to any intimate relationship unless I plan to be monogamous. And as much as is practicable, I will become involved with the political process. These things have not been easy for me to conclude, but there will never be a peace of mind within me if I don't change to embrace the things that cause me stress and discomfort.

If I had to say a final word about change, I would say never be afraid to do it. Change is a growth process. Just as babies grow into adults, change is about mental/emotional growth. You wouldn't want to grow up in your physical body but keep the mind of a child; right? That is essentially what will happen if you refuse to change any part of your behavior that is not serving your greatest good. It may be uncomfortable, but positive change is for your own good.

IN CLOSING

I wish I could give a well written summation of what manhood is within the limited pages of this book. It's like trying to stuff the entirety of my knowledge, wisdom, and experiences in each line. It is impossible to adequately summarize the totality of an individual's character, values, flaws and all, in any limited amount of space. There is so much more that could be said of the subject that this conversation could go on forever. It's about growth; and since growth is perpetual, this dialogue should be never ending, at least in theory anyway.

As I said in the opening pages, manhood is something we must define for ourselves. There is no real right or wrong in our efforts to give a value and meaning to manhood; more like best practice measures. It was my goal in this discourse to share my values, views, and opinions with my children in hopes that I could put back some of the missing elements that under other circumstances would have been there. I'm sharing with them now the things I should have been giving them all along. So, as I conclude this exchange, I'd like to say a personal word to all my sons.

I can only wonder what kind of man each one of you thinks I am. By the same token, I sit and try to imagine what type of men each of you are. There has been so much time and distance between us, I imagine it is probably hard for you all to understand why our situation had to be what it is. For that, I take full responsibility. In my youthful foolishness I was not able to see how my actions, or inactions, would affect us all in the long run. I have made some very poor judgment calls in the past, all which have set poor examples and established a reputation that I am not very proud of.

I have had a very long time to think about what I did right in my past; also, what I did wrong, and what I can do better. Each time I reevaluate my life, I come to the same conclusion; I don't want to be who I have been, but I want to be the man that I spoke of in these pages. I understand that I am in control of making that happen, so I plan to live in a way that dignifies and exemplifies that I am serious about what I say.

I own you all an apology that is long overdue which no amount of words would be meaningful enough to express. However inadequate they are, at present, they are all I have to express my deep sorrow. I did not want to turn out to be the type of father I have been over the last decade. I have fallen short on many fronts insofar as my responsibilities are concerned. I hope that each of you will find it in

131

your hearts to forgive me for all my shortcomings at some point. The man I am today is the man I should have been long before now, except, I would not be who I am if it were not for what I've been through. I just regret that it had to be at the expense of each of your childhoods.

I am so very proud of the men you all have become. I know life has not been a bed of roses, but you all have endured well and have each become men of distinction with whom I am blessed to have the fortune of being connected. If I had to choose one thing in life that has given me the most joy, it would be the gift of fatherhood; one that, based on my own actions, I don't really deserve. I appreciate more than you'll ever know your willingness not to hold my faults and shortcomings against me.

I understand that as we continue to grow together, we will have to acknowledge and confront our own and each other's imperfections. It is in my heart to be a solid and stable place of mental and emotional support that will help you work through the things that pain you. When holes are left because of something so significant as having a displaced parent, it is not an easy condition to fix. I pledge to do all in my power to be one person that you can count on loving you no matter what we have to face from here on.

The men that you have become, I will love no matter what. I may not always agree with your decisions, but I will always love and respect you for who you are. Throughout my time away, I have stayed awake many nights reflecting, planning, preparing and sometimes saddened to tears about the greatest loss of all—my sons. Life has presented us many highs, lows, joys and pains. My next challenge going forward is to make sure the pain of our past will not return void.

I want to leave a legacy very different from the past I'm currently recognized for. It has not been a flattering one. However, if I'm blessed with longevity of days, I believe I can and will establish a track record that my children and family can be proud of. In fact, I know I can. I have not been such a bad guy before now, and these last ten years have helped me mold myself into a better person. I assure you that as we continue to grow through manhood from now on in our lives, I will make every effort to be the man and example I've explained throughout this book; the man I know you all need and I know I should be.

Words are an insufficient expression of love. To me, love is best defined by your actions. Your actions are the only real and true expression of love. Because of our circumstances, it has been almost impossible for me to express the love I feel the way I want to, but if we were to use actions as a measure of love, I could only hope that you all will receive the labor that I have spent in compiling this

132

glimpse into me, as a small symbol of how much I do love each of you. Be it God's will, and by you all's acceptance, I will have a second opportunity to share with you the man I am today and the man I'll grow to be tomorrow. I love you!

ACKNOWLEDGMENTS

First, I would like to thank the Creator. It is by His grace that we are able to enjoy the many wonderful things about life. My mother, Tracie Taylor. You never gave up on me and managed to love me even when I was unlovable like only a mom could. My father, Raymond Dandridge. I'm sure you wish I would have listened more along the way, but as you always say, there are no mistakes. I heard you then, but I'm listening to you now. Although it may have seemed like it at times, your counsel didn't fall on deaf ears.

Very special thanks are due to you Vivian Neuman, my unofficial personal assistant. Without you I would have never been able to do this. You are an angel. Kenneth 'Shaq' Fuller for putting me in touch with Vivian. I owe you one big, homie. Paul Johnson, the literary genius; thank you so much for all your countless hours of mentoring about the publishing game and how to do it from the prison cell. Kevin E. Dolphin and the Cook City family. His sister Dorothy M. Scott. I'm looking forward to us building an empire in the years to come. To my Street Luv Team, A. 'Finesse' Witfeld, CEO of Street Luv Productions and his wife Liz Rodriquez. It won't be long now. The future is ours. In five years, the hood will know who runs the Streets—Street Luv is where it's at. My editor Ben Sorrell. I couldn't have done it without your red pen. If there are any mistakes, it's probably because I didn't listen to you. Marvin Clowney at M2 Graphics Studio for coming through in the clutch. Oh yeah, Trenell 'Uncle Chuck' Murphy, I ain't forget you family. We on teams now 'Dug' haha!

Frank West Jr., I'll never forget the time you told Ms. Johnson, "splitting us up would be like splitting up brothers." You always pressed 5, kept a few dollars on the books and never broke your word. Now that's real. I love you big bro. Arleen Aponte, what can I say? You may not have done it when I wanted, but you always came through; even if it was two years later. The *quiero mucho mamita*. Quentin Snead, Terrance Singleton, Wei Shi, Fernando Punett, Raphel Vaca, Ismael 'Chapo' Sanchez, Counselor Royer, all my English teachers and my family. Each of you has added something special to the last decade of my life.

I want to give a very special thanks to Lamar Culpepper. You were a major help in a time of need with the revised edits. Tobi Bowen who is a genius at branding and marketing. Thank you immensely for all your input on how to work social media and not giving up. It was invaluable and at just the right time. Margie Dunki-Jacobs, what can I say!?!? You inspired me to new levels of confidence and belief in what is possible with this book. Your time, your enthusiasm and pure loving energy have filled me up so much that I believe now more than ever in this project's purpose and meaning. Love you guys!

I also want to thank all the women who have touched my life on an intimate level. Each of you has added some very special element that has helped evolve me into the man I am today. I will never forget the sacrifices you all have made in helping cultivate me from a boy to a man. It was an investment that came at great personal sacrifice that I am forever indebted to you for having made.

And last, but not least, to my fair-weather friends and frenemies, thank you all. Your neglect, jealousy, envy and hate in some cases have been my motivation. I love you guys. You'll be the reason I succeed. Peace!

GETTING CONNECTED WITH CHABLIS

Speaking Engagements + Community Involvement

If you would like to book Chablis for speaking engagements, or If you're an individual who would be like to be part of a community that cares and you wants to make a difference, please reach out as follows:

Email: TheRealChablis@gmail.com

Facebook: facebook.com/ChablisD

Instagram: @TheRealChablis

Website: ChablisDandridge.com

Individuals Who Are Currently Incarcerated

If you are currently incarcerated and interested in connecting to a community of caring individuals and would like to transform your journey now, please reach out to bthestand@gmail.com

If you would like to continue the conversation, log on to chablisdandridge.com and download the PDF of the discussion question for FREE.

Made in the USA
Columbia, SC
11 June 2020